From Diamond Sculls to
Golden Handcuffs

From Diamond Sculls to Golden Handcuffs

A History of Rowe & Pitman

ANDREW LYCETT

ROBERT HALE · LONDON

© *Andrew Lycett 1998*
First published in Great Britain 1998

ISBN 0 7090 6301 6

Robert Hale Limited
Clerkenwell House
Clerkenwell Green
London EC1R 0HT

The right of Andrew Lycett to be identified as author of this work has been asserted by him in accordance with the Copyright, Designs and Patents Act 1988.

2 4 6 8 10 9 7 5 3 1

Typeset by
Derek Doyle & Associates, Mold, Flintshire.
Printed in Great Britain by
St Edmundsbury Press Limited, Bury St Edmunds
and bound by
WBC Book Manufacturers Limited, Bridgend

Contents

Acknowledgements   7
List of Illustrations   9

1 The Rowing Establishment   11
2 The Old School Tie   27
3 After the War   36
4 The Camp Bird   54
5 Stifling Red Tape   64
6 Moving On   75
7 New Broom   92
8 Searching for Partners   109
9 Into the Nineties   126

Appendices   146
Index   155

Acknowledgements

WRITING THE BIOGRAPHY of one of the most successful authors of all time led to this history of one of London's most interesting stockbrokers. But then Ian Fleming used to be a partner, and, as this book shows, Rowe & Pitman was always a bit like that – a firm that combined widespread connections with imaginative solutions.

So many thanks to Oliver Baring for taking the plunge and asking me to write this volume. I enjoyed working with him and with his distinguished executive committee of ex-partners – Peter Wilmot-Sitwell, David Brooke and James Ogilvy. In addition both Nigel Elwes and John Littlewood offered important help and advice.

Over the past couple of years, I have spoken to scores of people. I would particularly like to acknowledge the contributions of Bill Corney (a mine of information about the early days of Rowe & Pitman), Alan Hurst Brown, James D'Albiac, David Russell, Stuart Stradling, Geoffrey Finn (who made sure that the details about gilts were correct), Jim Graham-Watson and Ro Wadham. Several other people heeded my call for papers, photographs and anecdotes. In this context I would like to thank Peter Heming Johnson, Denis Milne, Peter Thompson, Alan Davenport, David Innes, George Pilkington, Adrian Philips, Fred Chitty, John Lewington, Michael Franzman, Sir Peter Vanneck, Peter Hardy, Will Robins, Andrew Martin Smith, Thelma Joel, Pauline Phillips, B.M. McCloy, Dennis Wade, Ellen Harvey, A.J. Hargrave, David Stobart, W.B. Nicholas, R.A. Page,

Adrienne Nash, L.M.V. Richards, June Baker, Keith Penfold, Valerie Warner, Cyril Cook, Don Harrison and Dora Hancock.

In addition, reminiscences of Rowe & Pitman were provided by Harry Oppenheimer, Julian Ogilvie Thompson, Sir David Scholey, Michael Verey, Mrs Peter Henderson and Jemima Pitman.

Dr David Stafford of the University of Edinburgh shared useful historical references, while Dr David Kynaston, historian of the City of London, was generous with his suggestions. The Beaverbrook Library at the House of Lords Records Office and the Guildhall Library were the repositories of useful supplementary material. My thanks also to Richard Roberts, historian and keeper of the archives at Schroders.

Finally, I would like to thank Oliver Baring's very efficient secretary, Olivia Tidmarsh, for her help in ensuring the project ran smoothly.

Andrew Lycett
January 1998

Illustrations

Between pages 96 and 97

1 George Rowe
2 Fred Pitman
3 Lancy Hugh Smith's XI at Mount Clare 1912 including Lancy Hugh Smith, Harry Little, Tommy Britton and W.T. Craven
4 Cricket at Titsey Place in the early 1950s including Wilfred de Knoop, Hilary Bray and Constant Rayment
5 Lancy Hugh Smith
6 Hugo Pitman
7 Fitz Graham Watson
8 Arthur Anderson
9 & 10 Smith and Nephew: Julian Martin Smith and Nigel Elwes
11 & 12 Baring and Son: Esmond Baring and Oliver Baring
13 Nick Verey presenting Peter Wilmot-Sitwell with an Augustus John portrait of Hugo Pitman on his retirement
14 Queen Elizabeth the Queen Mother visiting Woolgate House, November 1971. Also in picture: Bill Mackworth-Young, James Ogilvy, Peter Vanneck and Julian Martin Smith
15 Denis Milne
16 David Innes
17 Alan Hurst-Brown
18 Ian Fleming
19 Peter Wilmot-Sitwell
20 James Ogilvy
21 David Brooke
22 James D'Albiac
23 Signing an agreement with J. Sainsbury
24 The Operations Room in the mid-1970s

1 The Rowing Establishment

Rowe & Pitman's starting date is usually given as 1895, the year of the great boom in South African 'Kaffir' mining shares. But while its initial account was settled on 16 January 1895, its first dozen bargains were actually struck three weeks earlier on 27 December 1894. These showed the new firm setting off as it intended to carry on: at the forefront of then current market sentiment, acquiring for its clients a significant number of foreign mining shares – two purchases of Buffelsdoorn, and one each of Sutherland Reefs, Great Boulder and Cecil Rhodes's Chartered Company in that first dozen – plus a couple of US railroad stocks.

The original partners could not have picked a more lively time to establish a new firm of stockbrokers. In 1895 the London market finally threw off the depression of the early years of the decade, when negative reverberations from the Barings crash of 1890 still dominated the financial arena. In 1895 South African mining shares took off and the bedlam of the 'Kaffir Circus' spilled out onto the steps of the Stock Exchange building in Capel Court. Round the corner in Angel Court, a new club 'for financial men' opened on the back of the boom market. Officially called the City Athenaeum, it was known less formally as the Thieves' Kitchen. An early member was Barney Barnato, one of a colourful new breed of financiers who were challenging accepted City values. Born Barnett Isaacs in the East End of London, his Johannesburg Consolidated Investments was one of the main speculative vehicles of the time.

From Diamond Sculls to Golden Handcuffs

True to form, the market, the Stock Exchange, was an early indicator that the aristocratic ascendancy of Victorian days was passing. Quite why George D. Rowe and Fred Pitman were attracted to this particular City niche is not recorded. Both came from old-fashioned professional families, with links to two of the most important regional commercial centres of the North-west and Scotland. Rowe's father was a wealthy Liverpool businessman, while Pitman was one of eight sons (an entire boat, he liked to boast) of a prominent Writer to the Signet, or solicitor, in Edinburgh.

Rowing, indeed, was the spirit that brought the two men together, and carried the firm through its formative years. Rowe, from Marlborough and University College, Oxford, had participated in the University Boat Race in 1879 and 1880 (on the second occasion as President of the winning crew), while Pitman, a product of Eton and Trinity College, was stroke of a powerful Cambridge eight which recorded two victories in three outings between 1884 and 1886.

Aged thirty-six in 1895, the tall, distinguished-looking Rowe was the older of the two original partners. He had spent some time at the stockbroker W.H.L. Barnett and Company, while 31-year-old Fred Pitman had started his broking career with Panmure Gordon. Both brought useful business contacts to their new venture. Rowe's brother-in-law was Wilfrid Loder, a partner in the well-established private bank, Prescott, Cave, Buxton, Loder and Company, which had operated from Threadneedle Street since 1766. Later part of the National Westminster Bank, this establishment, which had become Prescott, Dimsdale, Cave, Tugwell and Company as a result of a merger in 1890, acted as the new firm's bankers and helped generate business.

Pitman came from the Scottish establishment, where he enjoyed excellent connections with the Edinburgh legal profession. His father, Frederick Pitman, worked for the Edinburgh solicitors J. and F. Anderson, headed by his uncle, John Anderson. In 1890 Fred junior had married Helen, the daughter of James Auldjo Jamieson, Writer to the Signet and senior partner in another major Scottish solicitor, Tods Murray and

The Rowing Establishment

Jamieson. Both these legal firms were to play significant roles in the development of Rowe & Pitman. Indeed, on its first day of operation, the new stockbroker received most of its business from Tods Murray and Jamieson whose influence north of the border was celebrated (along with the Pitman family's) in a popular rhyme – which was sung long before similar words about the Cabots, the Lowells and the city of Boston:

> *I've just come back from Auld Reekie*
> *From Jamieson, Murray and Tod,*
> *Where Blackburn speaks only to Pitman,*
> *And Pitman speaks only to God.*

In view of Rowe & Pitman's later prominence in mining finance, it is tempting to suggest that it was on the inside track of the Kaffir and related 'Westralian' booms of the mid-1890s. But evidence to support this is sketchy. More realistically, Rowe & Pitman anticipated the coming together of South African and American mining interests. Acting with the issuing house Anthony Gibbs and Sons, it took a small interest in the later successful Camp Bird mine in Colorado in 1900, where J.B. Robinson, an early South African mining magnate, and Marks Bulteel, another broker specializing in Kaffirs, had considerably higher stakes. Camp Bird was promoted by the Venture Corporation, one of the many dubious promotion vehicles which thrived in the market after the Kaffir boom had peaked.

Otherwise Rowe & Pitman played a peripheral role in the turn-of-the century mining bonanza. More typically, we find Fred Pitman coming before the Stock Exchange's General Purposes Committee in January 1903 to explain the background to the flotation of one of the firm's earliest corporate clients, the Federal Supply and Cold Storage Company of South Africa. Legal difficulties had caused the issue to be delayed, and the company wanted to know its position if it were to issue a second prospectus. Pitman appeared with 'some representatives of the market', described in the Committee's minutes as 'Mssrs Bendall (G. Kitchen and Co) and A. Gibbs'. As a leading jobber, George

Kitchin – the correct spelling – had been responsible for two of Rowe & Pitman's initial twelve bargains. With Wedd Jefferson and Company, another name on that list, Kitchin worked closely with Rowe & Pitman for many years.

Generally, building up the new firm was a steady, unspectacular process. The first business it brought to the market was the M. Hyam Wholesale Clothing Company in May 1897. Dating from the same year, another early corporate client was Thomas Tilling, which at the time was a family-owned omnibus company offering horses and carriages for hire. Its regular expansion into a diversified conglomerate over the next three-quarters of a century provided exactly the sort of reliable core income on which a stockbroker thrives.

Two important early sources of business were the River Plate and General Investment Trust and the London Trust. These came through the extended rowing network or, specifically, through Malcolm Pilkington, a slightly younger Etonian who had been in the Oxford crews of 1893-5. Known as 'Moppy', Pilkington joined Rowe & Pitman straight from university, initially as a half-commission man but later, from 1899, as a full partner. His connections played an important part in the development of the firm. The two investment trusts were chaired by his brother, Charlie, who had his own firm of jobbers specializing in South American railway stocks. As a member of the Lancashire glass manufacturing family, he attracted business from the Northwest, and in particular from Liverpool. In addition, a friend of his was Assistant Manager of Barclay's Bank in Cambridge. This introduced Rowe & Pitman to university clients – because of their recurring needs, another much-valued stock-broking staple. The university itself used Rowe & Pitman, as did King's College and, more long-standingly, the newly established ladies' 'hall', Girton.

Important though Pilkington was to the early development of Rowe & Pitman's business, it is no disrespect to his memory to say that he was overshadowed by the redoubtable Lancelot Hugh Smith, who had become a partner three years earlier, in 1896. On the surface, Hugh Smith was simply a scion of a well-known banking family, whose Smith's Bank, originally established in Nottingham in the late seventeenth century, was soon to be taken over by the Union Bank of London, before being absorbed, like Prescott Cave, Buxton, Loder and Company, into the National Westminster Bank.

In fact Lancy, as he was known, stood at the epicentre of a powerful City clique, including both family and friends, whose influence was probably more wide-ranging than even the established banks. In bald terms, he was the third son of Hugh Colin Smith, who in 1897, the year after Lancy joined Rowe & Pitman, became Governor of the Bank of England. As intelligent bankers, the Smiths had integrated successfully into the English aristocracy for nearly two centuries, while taking care all the while to nurture and maintain their roots in the City.

While the Smiths already had several influential branches, Lancy's closest relatives had created a formidable dynastic nexus in their own right, bringing together Smith with Grenfell, Hambro, Morgan and later (to a lesser extent) Baring family and business interests. The key building block in this framework was the Hugh Smiths themselves (as if to demonstrate their difference from other Smiths, they added their father's Christian name to their own surname). Lancy's eldest brother, Vivian, joined Morgan Grenfell and rose to become its senior managing director. Owen remained in charge of the family business as Chairman of Hay's Wharf. The tough, intellectually rigorous John straddled City and business worlds as both Managing Director of Hambros Bank and Chairman of the British Metal Corporation. The two remaining brothers, Aubrey and Humphrey, opted for the Navy, where they both became admirals. Of the sisters, Olive married into the Baring family, while Mildred was the wife of Sydney Buxton, the Liberal MP who was appointed Governor-General of South Africa. Lancy would doubtless have been satisfied that Mildred's daughter was later the Duchess of Grafton.

John Hugh Smith's appointment as Managing Director of Hambros Bank only emphasized the 'cousinhood'. For by then the Smiths and Hambros had cemented an all-embracing relationship which was to feature strongly, not only in the City generally, but in the history of Rowe & Pitman in particular. The liaison began when Hugh Colin Smith's first cousin Martin Ridley Smith married a Scots woman called Emily Stuart. At Cambridge Martin's brother Francis had been the best friend of Everard Hambro, scion of the emerging banking family. Through his brother, Martin also became a close friend of Everard's. When he invited Everard to stay with him in Scotland, the Hambro heir met and fell in love with his host's sister-in-law, Emily Ridley Smith's sister Mary, whom he married in 1866. In this way Martin Ridley Smith and Everard Hambro became brothers-in-law. But their links grew closer when two of the Ridley Smiths' daughters, Sybil and Winifred, married the Hambros' sons Eric and Olaf. Meanwhile a Hambro daughter Violet married the Ridley Smiths' son Everard (who, true to form, took the surname Martin Smith) to create one of the tightest family dynasties in the City.

The pact-making did not stop there. In Prince's Gate, London, the Everard Hambros lived next door to the Hugh Colin Smiths, and in turn became close friends. In 1871 these two immediate families decided to rent Mount Clare, an Adam house in Roehampton on the edge of Richmond Park, as their joint summer residence. Another prominent City figure with a summer house nearby was the American banker J. Pierpont Morgan, who was developing the British side of the family bank which had financed America's railroads. Inevitably the Morgans soon knew the Hugh Smiths and the Hambros extremely well. At Cambridge (an important location in this emerging saga) Everard's son Eric was the best friend of J. Pierpont Morgan's nephew, Walter Burns, a leading light in Morgan Grenfell, as the British side of the Morgan Bank was known after 1910, and where Hugh Colin Smith's son Vivian had recently been made a partner. (In 1941, three years after being ennobled as Lord Bicester, he became Senior Managing Director, or Chairman.) To strengthen the ties even more, both Everard Hambro and Hugh Colin Smith served as directors of the Bank of England (before the latter became Governor). And Everard's son Eric was the man who married Sybil Ridley Smith.

The Rowing Establishment

Inevitably Lancy's network of contacts extended further afield. On a family level, his sister Olive's marriage gave him contacts in the Baring banking family. His mother was Constance Adeane, daughter of another director of the Bank of England, whose sister had married into the Grenfell banking family. At Fruhling and Goschen, Lancy had worked closely with his cousin Dick Grenfell, whose father, Teddy, became J. Pierpont Morgan's English partner. Another cousin, Robert Newman, became Governor of the Bank of England in 1896. There was even a further Smith-Hambro connection in that Audrey Martin Smith, sister of Sybil and Winifred, married Walter Heriot, a partner in the bank that was then still officially known as C.J. Hambro and Son.

Ironically, when Lancy Hugh Smith told his father he wanted to become a stockbroker, he was not taken seriously. The Stock Exchange was not considered a suitable career for a Smith. However, after leaving Eton (a schooling that was fast becoming *de rigueur* at Rowe & Pitman), Lancy had spent a short period as a fledgling banker both with the family concern in Derby and with Fruhling and Goschen in the City, and had heartily disliked that career. As a compromise, his father tried to direct him to joining Mullen's, the government broker, where the Senior Partner, Henry Daniell, was a Smith cousin, but there were no openings.

So, *faute de mieux*, Lancy was plunged into stockbroking – an inspired choice because his sociable but inherently snobbish personality was eminently suited to developing the personal contacts that were necessary for success. More than ever in those days, stockbroking was a matter of who one knew. A few clerks ran the office, one partner perhaps was unlucky enough to have to spend time on the floor of the Exchange, while the ones with connections donned their top hats and went off every morning to brief their friends and lobby for business in the partners' rooms of the great banks and other emerging financial institutions.

Of his early days, Lancy has recorded:

> I used to go to Goschens first thing every day. At that time all the partners in the big houses used to enjoy having little 'specs', and the South African boom, which was an orgy of speculation, was

just drawing to an end. There was also a very big market in American Rails. The New York Market, which settled each day for cash, drove some of their gamblers to London, where they could buy for the Account, sometimes a fortnight or three weeks on. This gave them a good run for their money.

I used to get my prices at 10.45, which were based on the New York closing, and again at 3, when New York came on – that was 10 a.m. New York – and run round to Morgan's with them.

With his ties with Hambros and Morgan's, Lancy was a great catch for Rowe & Pitman's new firm. Indeed, Rowe got the idea of 'conscripting' Lancy from seeing him lunching with Walter Burns. He did not approach him directly, however. As another example of how the City – and society – worked at that time, Rowe asked his friend Walter Cunliffe to enquire of his friend Hugh Colin Smith whether young Lancy could join the firm. Cunliffe, whose family ran an accepting house, was then a director of the Bank of England and later went on to become Governor. Apart from his connection with Burns and the Morgans, Lancy had the added attraction in Rowe's eyes of not being a 'wet bob'. He had no interest in rowing, and could be relied upon to keep the office going when his fellow partners were engaged in other serious pursuits, such as Henley week.

Nevertheless it took some time for Lancy's relatives and friends to orientate their business to Rowe & Pitman. Until after the First World War, Hambros continued to use de Zoete's. Baring's had their existing brokers, and anyway Lancy failed to impress their chairman, Lord Revelstoke. Even Morgan's, the most promising of the Hugh Smith stable of connections, was initially hesitant to use Rowe & Pitman.

Lancy used to say that his great break came in 1898 when, against his wishes, he accompanied Walter Burns to the United States.

I was away four months, and going there 'made' me, as I made friends with the then young J.P. Morgan, who shortly after came to the London office, where he stayed many years. I consider my connection with Morgan's as the most important link that Rowe & Pitman have made in its history. It did not come at all at once – as in every case they had their own brokers. Morgan's had Marks Bulteel and Panmure Gordon, and until Koch, the chief partner in Panmure Gordon died, Rowe & Pitman were never brokers to a Morgan issue, and there were many in those days, for the US Railways were always making issues of bonds, and placing what they could in London. I remember being very hurt that we could not get in, but J.S. Morgan and Co were quite right. After the war when Koch died, and Fleischman of Messels had to leave the Stock Exchange because of his German origin, Rowe & Pitman had their chance.

In a very short time Lancy was one of the best-known and respected figures on the Exchange. His strength was that, despite – or perhaps because of – his connections, he knew what he was talking about. In January 1899 his fellow brokers Smith St Aubyn were doing business with Speyers, a small merchant bank, 'on introduction of Lancelot H. Smith'. In October 1900 he helped form the London Cremation Company, which owned the Golders Green Crematorium and was chaired by his cousin Everard Martin Smith. When the same year Anthony Gibbs experienced doubts about its Camp Bird investment, it called in its two brokers Arthur Wagg of Helbert Wagg and Lancy Smith of Rowe & Pitman. After Wagg, a Rothschild relative whose firm often acted for Rothschild interests, stated unconvincingly that he did not understand 'latter-day finance', it was left to Lancy to 'explain the matter'. In 1907 Morgans was advising its Paris branch about two leading brokers in London: 'Panmure Gordon are probably the most important firm here and Rowe & Pitman are very conservative and active Brokers.'

Arthur Wagg attributed this to Lancy's 'flair', rather than to any innate brilliance. Referring to Lancy, his friend Wagg later recorded:

> I have never known anyone who had so many friends or so many enemies. One could not be indifferent to him. The number of his

enemies is perhaps not surprising, for he took no trouble whatever to win the good opinion of anybody in whom he was not interested. . . .

His faults were apparent the very first time one saw him. One resented the somewhat supercilious manner in which he took stock of one. One resented, possibly, his talk about the great people he knew, and who possibly one did not know oneself. One had probably heard of his success in business, and his prosperity, and many people doubtless resented that as well. . . .

He certainly has not got the ability of several other members of his family. He had no great patience with detail, but he had great flair. He seemed to possess the gift of being able to 'smell out' that a security was attractive before it ever occurred to other people. The second reason for his success was undoubtedly the devotion of so many friends; and the third reason was that he came of a large family, not only of brothers, but of cousins, first, second and third. He possessed a great feeling of loyalty towards all these relations, and if there was an attractive vacancy, Lancie [sic] always knew of some cousin or other who could fill it, and what is more, I never heard of a single case where his recommendation did not turn out satisfactorily.

To his dying day Lancy remained a bachelor, and a crusty one at that. But he was not impervious to the charms of women, though to describe him as romantic would be stretching the point. At one stage he was keen on his cousin Violet Hambro. But when she unexpectedly opted to marry another cousin, Everard Martin Smith, in 1906, he began looking to the *demimonde* for female company and took up with a chorus girl called Jean Rhys (later widely known as a novelist). She was just nineteen (less than half his age) and working in a West End musical when she met him at a supper party in 1910. She wrote that she disliked him at first but came to adore him, seeing him as a symbol of all the rich, dashing men she had read about in books about London.

For eighteen months they were lovers, during which time Lancy paid for her singing and dancing lessons. At some stage she also met Julian Martin Smith who clearly disapproved of his cousin's liaison. He encouraged Lancy to break off the relationship – whereupon, out of genuine heartbreak, she wilfully went and got herself pregnant by another man. Lancy encouraged her to have the child and offered to help. She almost convinced herself that she was having Lancy's baby. But worry about the affair seems to have affected his health, and once again Julian stepped in to extricate his older cousin. He gave Jean Rhys some gold, sewn in a little canvas bag. Although he was courteous, Rhys never forgave him and portrayed him as slick, supercilious and exploitative in her 1934 novel *Voyage in the Dark*. Lancy, by contrast, comes out well from this and other of her writings: he is attractive and sensitive. He gave her an allowance until 1919, when she went to the Continent. They met a couple of times during the 1920s, when she needed money, and were in touch again at the end of the decade – an experience she used to paint a picture of the more mature, and somewhat smugger Lancy in her novel *After Leaving Mr Mackenzie*. (Lancy's youngest brother also enjoyed a famous literary liaison. John, later Managing Director of Hambros, was a close friend of the American author Edith Wharton.)

While the private Lancy had redeeming elements (he ended his life with twenty-eight godchildren), in the office he was a martinet. Staff, and particularly the young boys, were treated like serfs. His copy of *The Times* had to be ironed each day. When one unfortunate lad had the audacity to eat an orange in the office, Lancy ordered Palmer, the office manager, to dismiss the offender instantly.

Lancy's skills were in wheeling and dealing, rather than man management. Even so, Rowe & Pitman's growth was slow. Capitalized at £10,000, the firm's gross commissions for its first six months in 1895 were £4,531. Investment and other income raised this side of the balance sheet to £5,024, from which £691 had to be deducted for expenses, leaving £4,333 to be divided between what were then only two partners – nevertheless, a healthy return in anyone's book. Commissions for the full year of 1895 were £9,980, a figure that was not bettered until 1899.

Even in 1900, commissions for the whole years had risen only to £15,116, while expenses were now running at £3,725, and there were four partners – Rowe, Pitman, Hugh Smith and Pilkington – to share the profits. (Lancy initially had 6 per cent of the business. This was to rise to 38½ per cent in 1930 before settling back to 28 and then 24 per cent following the appointment of additional partners in the middle of the decade.)

During its first five years, the firm had offices on the second floor at 50 Threadneedle Street, next door to another stockbroker called Cazenove & Akroyd. Appropriately the telegraphic address was REMIGIUM, the collective Latin word for oarsmen. But conditions were cramped as well as primitive. Lancy's joining the firm was delayed while the partners found a table for him to sit at. And there was no lift or lavatory. As a result even Lancy, who was not known to care much about the problems of the working classes, was wont to wonder, he later admitted, which unfortunate clerk had the responsibility of emptying the office chamber-pot that was kept in a cupboard in the shorthand writer's room.

No one was surprised that the firm lost little time in moving to 117 Bishopsgate Within in 1900, and then, as business improved and the number of staff increased, continued to change offices fairly frequently, decamping to 14 Austin Friars in 1902, and then again eight years later to the newly constructed Pinners Hall, also in Austin Friars, where Rowe & Pitman took the whole length of the basement.

Two important newcomers as partners in the early years of the new century were Guthrie Watson and Robert Cooper. Watson, a Cambridge friend of Lancy's, helped consolidate the firm's solid Scottish connections. His father had founded one of the biggest insurance companies north of the border, the Scottish Provident Institution, which was now managed by Guthrie's brother, James Graham Watson. The latter had married Charlotte Boothby, one of five sisters, another of whom was the wife of Walter Cunliffe. Their brother, Robert Boothby, was to follow James Graham Watson as manager of the Scottish Provident and later go on to become a director of the Bank of Scotland.

The Rowing Establishment

Guthrie himself had a relaxed attitude to stockbroking. He preferred fishing to the City, and would often leave at 11 a.m., telling his colleagues, 'I am going up West to take the dog for a walk.' (He had a flat in St James's Street.) He is remembered for his wit, which expressed itself in aphorisms: 'Don't be a tram, you must be a bus,' he would counsel members of staff, drawing, in fact, on Maurice Evan Hare's 1905 limerick:

> *There once was a man who said 'Damn!*
> *It is borne in upon me I am*
> *An engine that moves*
> *In predestinate grooves,*
> *I'm not even a bus, I'm a tram.'*

Nevertheless, there is no doubt that, following Guthrie Watson's accession to the partnership in 1902, valuable Scottish Provident business began to flow through Rowe & Pitman, which for some time was known in the City as the 'Scotch broker'. It was a sign of the times that insurance companies were becoming almost as important potential customers as banks. Insurance companies need to buy equities and gilts to satisfy the claims of a growing mass market. In this context, a valuable and much appreciated half-commission man for Rowe & Pitman was Frederick Balfour, whose father-in-law was Chairman of the Sun Insurance Company. Malcolm Pilkington cultivated this connection, which paid dividends later when he spotted the large sinking fund attached to the Bank of England's 3½ per cent Conversion, and was rewarded with the Sun's profitable order for £10 million worth.

Outside the day-to-day business with the banks, there was underwriting to be shared with other stockbrokers. Lancy's connections with Scrimgeours and Nivisons, which did London flotations for the Australian and other governments, were useful here. For the rest, Cunliffe Brothers was already a major corporate client, as was the dynamic and fast-growing merchant company Balfour Williamson – originally Liverpool-based (a Pilkington connection), but from 1909 headquartered in London and active in Latin America, where that year the city enjoyed its first serious profits from the oil business (in this case, in the shares of the Peru-based Lobitos Oilfields, an important Balfour Williamson interest).

Lancy's 1898 trip to the United States clearly paid dividends since Rowe & Pitman was increasingly involved with the New York market (and in arbitrage possibilities between there and London). However one such 'play' in April 1906 brought another hearing before the Stock Exchange's General Purposes Committee. The firm had bought $25,000 Shawinigan Water and Power Company 5% Consolidated First Mortgage Bonds at 101⅞ from Marnham and Company, the price in the official list being 101-103. But when the bonds were delivered, Marnham claimed it had been underpaid on the exchange rate. Rowe & Pitman argued that it had already billed its client at the lower rate, which was the one normally used in dollar bond transactions. However, when Marnham produced evidence that the Bond quoted the specific exchange rate of $500 or £102 14s 10d, the Committee found against Rowe & Pitman.

As it consolidated its position with increasing volumes of business in the early years of the century, Rowe & Pitman took on additional half-commission men. Although many of these passed quickly through the firm, one who deserves mention was Claud Serocold, a distant cousin of Lancy's. With few personal connections, Serocold was remembered at Rowe & Pitman for his involvement in an unsuccessful speculation with a German, which resulted in his having to leave. However there may have been more than a whiff of sour grapes in this memory. For Serocold had won the confidence of Walter Cunliffe, and when he joined a then moribund competitor, Cazenove & Akroyd in 1903, he not only took much of the lucrative Cunliffe Brothers business but also had the ear of the man who was to be Governor of the Bank of England. When Serocold subsequently became Senior Partner, Cazenove & Akroyd changed out of all recognition, so that fifty years later it was to rival Rowe & Pitman as the leading stockbroker in the City.

Walter White, from George Rowe's former firm, also started

The Rowing Establishment

as a half-commission man. He was so successful in one particular area of business – the market in government securities, or Consols, which was badly depressed around the turn of the century – that he was invited to become a full partner in 1917. It helped that his family cement business was one of the largest companies which merged into the Blue Circle group, a prominent Rowe & Pitman client later in the century.

Robert Cooper, the sixth of the pre-First World War partners, specialized in a different, but equally valuable, type of business. His entrée to the firm was his friendship with the sociable Malcolm Pilkington. But no one was under any illusion that his main asset was that his father managed the office of Charles Morrison, the richest man in England. Cooper drove a hard bargain when he joined in 1906: he would receive 62.5% of all Morrison commissions. Rowe & Pitman quickly began acting for Morrison, whose family had grown rich in the textile business. And before long the close connection paid off handsomely, since Morrison died in 1909, and Rowe & Pitman was appointed to handle his estate, which was provisionally valued at £12 million. Commissions that year were a handsome £55,267, of which Cooper took £11,133. In his will Charles Morrison left his sister Ellen £2 million. But she only survived him by two years, after which Rowe & Pitman was called upon to handle her estate as well. For many years afterwards, the bulk of the Morrison family's Stock Exchange dealings passed through the firm.

The last of the seven pre-war partners never had the opportunity to prove his mettle (in the City, that is). He was Lancy's cousin, Julian Martin Smith, who joined the firm straight from Eton and Trinity College Cambridge, in 1909, and became a partner four years later. Julian was the archetypal gilded Edwardian youth. The son of Martin Ridley Smith, he was invested with charm, looks and a certain impulsiveness. A revealing story told of him is that, seeing the poor results in the contract book one day, he returned immediately to the Stock Exchange. Hailing two of the biggest jobbers on the Consol market, he put through a deal with both of them that showed an immediate £100 profit.

Julian was just finding his way in the City when war broke

out. One of the first men to join up, he was commissioned as a second lieutenant in the Intelligence Department and was attached to the 9th (Queens Royal) Lancers. Very early in the conflict, on 7 September 1914, he was taking part in the actions which later became known as the Battle of the Marne when he was hit in the spine by a shell splinter and died two days later.

When Lancy heard the news, he observed that 'for a long time the sun went out of my life, and out of many others'. Unconsciously he echoed the words of the Foreign Secretary, Sir Edward Grey, who little more than a month beforehand, had famously declared, 'The lamps are going out all over Europe. We shall not see them lit again in our lifetime.'

2 The Old School Tie

IRONICALLY FOR A FIRM already noted for its Etonian connections, Rowe & Pitman could not have survived its first two decades without its Old Olavians. St Olave's School was a grammar school just across the river from the City, in Tooley Street, Bermondsey, and very close to Hay's Wharf, the Smith family business, which explains why Lancy's brother, John Hugh Smith, who had spent a short time at Rowe & Pitman, was a governor there. From 1893 to 1922 the school was excellently run by a great headmaster, William Rushbrooke, a classical scholar who was a friend of the Liberal Prime Minister, Herbert Asquith.

Well before the First World War it had become a habit, then a tradition, and finally almost a drawback (because it created a privileged 'freemasonry') to recruit Rowe & Pitman's clerks from St Olave's. The first Olavian to make his mark was the sort of exception that proves a rule. Normally these new employees came as young lads aged fourteen or fifteen. But when Harry Little arrived in July 1900, he was not only a Cambridge graduate but a 'Wrangler', as anyone who distinguishes himself by obtaining one of the top ten places in the Mathematical Tripos is called.

Little was hired by Lancy as a clerk in the American Department on a salary of £55 per annum. He joined a small staff headed by Tommy Britton, whom George Rowe had brought from his previous employers. At the very start the only two employees were Britton, who earned £250 a year as office manager, and young Joe Lovesay, who was paid 7s 6d a week as a general messenger-cum-dogsbody. Britton soon made his mark as a City character. Clean-shaven, with a ram's fleece of white woolly hair, gold-rimmed spectacles and the statutory stiff collar with rounded points, he recruited a dealer called W.T. Craven and two additional clerks called Mills and Battie.

Within a dozen years the staff had risen to twenty-two, serving the six partners. The rewards were not great: as a rule someone in his early twenties was paid between £50 and £70, someone a bit older £120. These salaries would increase by an average of £10 a year, while the young boys, on around 7s a week, were given a weekly increase of 1-2s, but were expressly not employed full time until they were earning the equivalent of more than £40 per annum. Holidays were more generous, with three weeks for those who had been with the firm five years and four weeks for those with twenty years' service.

Typists had their own salary scale. The first three, all male, were paid £104 a year irrespective of age. Women were only considered for the job after the outbreak of war when Miss Lovering was appointed on a weekly wage of £1 15s 0d. One of her male predecessors, Fred Jay, rose to the position of Senior Dealer, later becoming the first of several Rowe & Pitman clerks to be made a member of the Stock Exchange.

The first staff bonus scheme in 1908 was not a great success. The Senior Partner distributed the proceeds of a bag of gold coins to assembled staff – a fixed amount according to each member's length of service. A more realistic system, based on profits, was introduced two years later. Heads of departments received 20 per cent of their salary, others between 10 and 17 per cent according to salary, and this bonus, the precursor of the Staff Provident Fund, was paid regularly in January and June of each year.

After brief tenures at two other addresses, Rowe & Pitman first put down roots at 14 Austin Friars. Here the firm occupied the ground and basement floors – some 1,000 square feet in all. The general office occupied the front section of the ground floor, and behind this were two small rooms, one used as a waiting room and the other occupied by the two half-commission men of the time, Walter Grenfell and Frederick Balfour. The six partners sat in a room at the rear, with George Rowe and Fred Pitman facing each other at a traditional partners' desk; Lancy Hugh Smith and Pilkington were similarly seated, with Guthrie Watson and Robert Cooper at separate desks, with their backs to the others. The basement contained the typists' office, which also housed the post department. A strong-room, two store-rooms, a coal cellar and the wash place, with lavatories, were also located in the basement area.

The general office had five desks: a large one, weighed down with the ledgers, was used by anyone who came from the Exchange (or House) late in the afternoon; one was shared by the Manager and the Dividend Clerk; at another the contracts were made out and the American business attended to; and there were two others for the Transfer, Name and Jobbers departments.

To accommodate a growing volume of business, the transfer clerks at Austin Friars acquired the firm's first three-drawer filing cabinet. The filing was done by the senior boy, Ashman, who was known for his habit of riding his bicycle up the steps of the building and in as far as the half swing door at the entrance to this main office. A lance corporal in the Machine Gun Corps during the First World War, he remained with the firm until the 1950s.

Outgoing letters were copied in books, as were contract notes and statements. All books and ledgers were fully bound and stored in the strong-room. They were brought up each morning in a hand-wound lift. More immediate contact with the outside world was by way of two telephones in the general office. One, with the number CENtral 9503, was rented from the GPO and situated in a large, unglazed booth. The other, LONdon Wall 2409, was provided by the privately run National Telephone Company and found in a half-glazed box. In addition there was a direct line to the Stock Exchange, and a tape machine which recorded prices throughout the day. This contraption also divulged news of sporting fixtures, such as the University Boat Race, a facility which was much appreciated by the two original partners.

Every time a partner wanted to place an outside telephone call, he had to summon a boy, give the required number and await the connection. The boy was responsible for disconnecting at the end of the conversation. This was easy with the GPO line as a bell rang when the extension receiver was replaced. The other line depended on a visual indicator which was often not noticed, so that the next incoming call went straight through to a discomfited partner.

The offices were heated by large coal fires lit by the housekeeper, Ware, who occupied a flat at the top of the building. As Office Manager, Tommy Britton secured for himself the prime position next to the fire in the general office, where a large metal screen at the end of his desk served to protect him from scorching.

With few exceptions, the staff were in the office from 10 a.m. to 6 p.m., the actual pace of work being governed by the three settlement days in the fortnightly account – Contango, Ticket and Account days – when the pressure was so intense that tempers sometimes became frayed. One day in 1909, after a liquid lunch in the nearby Star and Cushion pub, several clerks actually staged a strike. This precipitate industrial action quickly ended. But, significantly, it was soon followed by the improved staff bonus scheme, together with a more proactive approach to industrial relations.

Generally, however, the atmosphere at Austin Friars was calmer. Britton was often the butt of good-natured office pranks. On one occasion a coconut was taken from his Gladstone bag, cut in two and carefully scraped out. After it had been refilled with lead paperweights, the two halves were rejoined and placed back in the bag. In another jape, a cheap alarm clock, which he had purchased from Pontings, was secretly set to go off during his train journey home.

Even this combination of well-trained, moderately happy staff and well-connected partners was not enough to protect Rowe & Pitman against occasional fraud. A bond dealer called W.D. Fisher was wont to use the firm as an intermediary to place good Canadian and American bonds with insurance companies. In 1907, in the normal run of business, Frederick Balfour, the half-commission man, sold some of these Canadian bonds to his friends in Sun Insurance. Unwisely, the firm had already paid Fisher against his receipt. Only later did it discover that there were no such bonds. Fisher bolted to the United States, £11,600 better off for his fraud. The only benefit from this unfortunate episode was that Rowe & Pitman became acquainted with another of Fisher's victims, Kissel Kinnicutt, which later became its chief correspondent for North American business.

A second 'sting' was more complicated and, to certain tastes, romantic. A promising young man called McCulloch Christison, an old boy of Dulwich College, had obtained a job as an authorized clerk in Rowe & Pitman's House Department. To an extent, he was a portage of Lancy's, since his father had been a fellow director with Hugh Colin Smith on the board of the Lebong Tea Company. One day he told Fred Pitman that he had met an old school friend who wanted to put some business through the firm. The friend's name was Francis Shackleton and he was the younger brother of the famous Antarctic explorer.

Further enquiries revealed that Shackleton was a friend and business partner of Lord Ronald Gower who, being both an Old Etonian and the younger brother of the Duke of Sutherland, seemed an ideal client to Pitman. On meeting the two men, Pitman learned that Lord Ronald wanted to buy into a company called Montevideo Improvements, and his initial order was for 5,000 shares. Although there was very little market in this stock, his lordship stated helpfully that a firm of brokers called Linton Clarke might have some for sale. Rowe & Pitman approached Linton Clarke and bought the shares, which were duly paid for by Gower.

Shortly afterwards Shackleton, who appeared to have authority from Gower, placed two more orders for shares in the same company. The firm went through the same process, and delivered the transfers to Lord Ronald. Only on these occasions there was no reply and no cheque. When Christison contacted his friend Shackleton, he was told not to worry: his lordship had gone abroad and the transfers had been forwarded to him. But when nothing further was heard, Lancy urged his partners

George Rowe and Fred Pitman to pay a visit on their friend Shackleton.

On going to his Park Lane flat – described by Lancy as 'one of those little houses with windows that I have always thought looked suspicious' – the two men were greeted by a servant and 'doctor' who told them Shackleton was ill and could see no one. The next day the brother of the great explorer had mysteriously disappeared.

Lord Ronald subsequently contacted Rowe & Pitman and said that, while he had given the order for the first tranche of shares, the two subsequent purchases were nothing to do with him. He claimed he had never given the firm authority to accept Shackleton's orders without his countersignature. In February 1911 Rowe & Pitman sued for the return of £10,000 and won. But since Lord Ronald declared himself bankrupt, very little in the way of assets was recouped.

During the court action, the bare bones of the scam were revealed. Having bought some worthless shares in Montevideo Improvements, Gower and his fellow crook instructed their banker, Cox and Company, to sell them. They gave their order to their broker, Linton Clarke, who predictably was unable to sell the stock until Rowe & Pitman emerged on the scene. 'We paid Linton Clarke – they paid Cox's,' recalled Lancy Hugh Smith. 'Cox's put the money to Shackleton's account, and Lord Ronald repudiated his bargain, and that was the plot, and a very clever one too.'

While this may have been so, it highlighted an inherent weakness in Rowe & Pitman. Most firms would have done the same, it is true, but Fred Pitman had been prepared to take Lord Ronald as a client simply because of his relationship to the richest Duke in Scotland. Some rudimentary homework would have revealed that Gower had a poor reputation, being associated with Queen Victoria's 'other' son, Prince Eddy of Connaught, in a louche homosexual set. With Shackleton, he was implicated in the theft of the Irish crown jewels from Dublin Castle, a homosexual scandal with such wide-reaching implications that the Vice-regal Commission appointed to examine it was promptly adjourned on the new King Edward V's orders, never to meet again. Shackleton himself had a long history of shady share promotion and later went to prison for fraud.

A third mishap was even closer to home. Arthur Grenfell, a friend of both Lancy and Malcolm Pilkington, was one of the eight sons of a merchant banker called Pascoe Grenfell. A lively and charming Old Etonian, he started his career as a clerk in Morgan's, where he seemed destined for great things. But when Jack Morgan took in Arthur's slightly older second cousin, E.C. (Teddy) Grenfell, as a steadying influence on Walter Burns, the headstrong Arthur took offence and decamped to Morton Rose, a small merchant bank where his father had been a partner. Having suffered in the economic recession which accompanied the 1890 Baring crisis, Morton Rose reinvented itself over the following years as Chaplin, Milne & Grenfell.

There Arthur flourished as a visionary financier, and might have risen to the very top of the City if he had not perennially seen the Stock Exchange as a vehicle for gambling. He might have survived even that, except that, as David Kynaston notes in his book *The City of London*, 'For him it was impossible that a swan could ever be a goose'. Arthur's first spectacular punt was on shares of the Aitcheson, Topeka and Santa Fe Railway in the United States. As these matured he called his shares and borrowed money on them, a process he repeated until he was sitting on a profit of some £250,000. At this stage his family intervened and forced him to bail out.

But Arthur was unable to resist the lure of a good-looking investment. After marrying a daughter of the Fourth Earl Grey in 1901, he continued to speculate with any money he could lay his hands on, including his £100,000 marriage settlement. As this became widely known, it rebounded on his firm. But such was his charm that his partners were unable to bring themselves to ask him to resign. He was only forced to give up his role as Managing Director.

Even at that stage, sympathy was with him. As Robert Benson, a close friend of Arthur's father-in-law, Lord Grey, wrote to Hugo Baring, a trustee of the marriage settlement,

[Arthur] has been as much sinned against as sinning. I feel very strongly about old and experienced brokers who let young men run up big a/cs, omit to advise – or even dissuade – sales and then put the knife in at the bottom. Arthur was 'fey', as most successful and courageous men have been once in their lives – and had temporarily lost his sense of proportion. His natural generosity also contributed.

Despite its own youthfulness as a firm, Rowe & Pitman may indeed have been one of the brokers which allowed Grenfell to continue running up his accounts. For Arthur had excellent contacts in mining exploration, particularly in southern Africa, where he was a director of United Africa Explorations and of the Charter Trust and Agency, established in 1902 to work on behalf of the British South Africa Company (where Lord Grey was Chairman). When his father-in-law moved to Canada as Governor-General in 1904, Arthur followed suit, establishing the Canadian Agency, a finance house specializing in Canadian securities in 1908.

At this stage, however, he ran foul of the powerful Hugh Smith axis. In order to finance the Agency he borrowed £100,000 from long-suffering friends. His undoing was to make a bargain with Lancy's elder brother Vivian, now with J.S. Morgan and Company, to purchase some of the Hugh Smith family land at Roehampton, where he himself had built a Lutyens-designed house. When Arthur went back on this deal Vivian was furious and Lancy resolved never to deal on his behalf again.

That did not prevent Rowe & Pitman losing money when various of Grenfell's Canadian and American investments went spectacularly wrong in May 1914, just before the start of the First World War. The firm was involved because, as part of its regular business, it loaned money to other brokers and jobbers. Among other accounts it had a loan with the reputable broking firm, Marks, Bulteel, Mills and Company. Julian Martin Smith was working with Walter White on the finance side of the business at the time, and he had lent Marks Bulteel a large sum against some ordinary stock in the Grand Trunk Railway, then priced at 18s.

But there was no reason to connect this with Arthur Grenfell, nor to doubt the credit of Marks Bulteel.

When the extent of Arthur's failure (around £3 million) became apparent, the Bank of England stepped in to mount a rescue operation. As part of this process George Rowe was visited by the Government Broker, Henry Daniel, and informed that Marks Bulteel had been let down by Grenfell and could not meet the differences. Daniel urged Rowe to take over the Grand Trunks at 18s, and so save Marks Bulteel and prevent a panic which would ruin many firms. With no choice in the matter, Rowe & Pitman agreed, but immediately cut the loss by selling at around 11s, or a loss of some £36,000.

Grenfell was subsequently declared bankrupt. After a 'good' war, he returned to the City determined to remake his fortune and to repay his creditors. Although he had some success in the first of these ambitions, it is not known whether Rowe & Pitman ever saw any payment on the IOU which Malcolm Pilkington had extracted from him.

3   After the War

ON FRIDAY, 31 JULY 1914, the Stock Exchange closed its doors until further notice, the bank rate was doubled and everyone prepared for war. Within days Julian Martin Smith was off to France with the British Expeditionary Force. Robert Cooper and Guthrie Watson followed him to the front. And in time Lancy also found himself a useful job. At the outbreak of hostilities he ostensibly held a commission as a lieutenant in the Westminster Dragoons, but there is no evidence that he saw any service with them. Instead he cultivated his political connections and occupied himself with what were later gazetted as 'special duties'.

In June 1915, he was appointed head of the British Mission to Sweden. The object of the exercise was to encourage the generally pro-German Swedes to remain as neutral as could be expected and, in particular, to deter them from impeding the free passage of goods to beleaguered Imperial Russia. To assist him in this task he made a point of asking Eric Hambro, his banker cousin, to join his four-man delegation. (The other members were Robert Vansittart from the Foreign Office and Hugh Cleminson, a commercial lawyer who had specialized in Scandinavia.) Taking Hambro was an astute move because, through his family, he enjoyed good relations with Knut Wallenberg, who had temporarily resigned as Chairman of Stockholms Enskilda Banken and was serving as Foreign Minister. Although the mission only lasted four months, it was widely judged a success and ensured that Lancy would spend three more years in quasi-secret activity on the fringes of intelligence and economic warfare.

After the War

Another of Lancy's successful wartime 'quangos' was the Board of Trade's Norwegian Fish Committee, where again he managed to co-opt his cousin Eric Hambro. This time the aim was to keep Norway's fish stocks from Germany. With the help of the newly formed British Bank of Northern Commerce (where Knut Wallenberg was the major shareholder), Hambro skilfully put together the finance required to purchase the fish outright. Lancy also acted as Chairman of the Tobacco and Matches Control Board (which proved useful for his post-war career), and as a member of the Admiralty's Interdepartmental Oil Committee and the Board of Trade's powerful Contraband Committee. For these services, he was awarded a CBE in June 1917.

Lancy was probably assisted by his brother Aubrey who, after serving as British Naval Attaché in Russia, Sweden and Norway from 1908 to 1912, had become the war-time Deputy Director of Naval Intelligence under Admiral Sir 'Blinker' Hall. (Another member of Hall's legendary Room 40 was Claud Serocold, now with Cazenove.) It cannot have held Lancy back either that he was now part of the political establishment. Winston Churchill, the First Lord of the Admiralty, later Minister of Munitions, had become a friend. In her unpublished autobiography, Lancy's mother, Constance Smith, recorded his observation in April 1916 that, since leaving office, Churchill had taken to painting. 'Lancelot likes Clementine extremely,' she added, referring to the politician's wife.

Given Lancy's penchant for feminine company, romantic souls have alighted on a clue in a letter from Prime Minister Herbert Asquith to his lover Venetia Stanley in March 1915 to suggest that there may have been another reason for Lancy's preferment. Writing from Walmer Castle, Asquith described a party: 'Of Lady Essex and Kitty there is nothing new to be said: and Margot's middle-aged young man, Lancelot Smith, is quite a chip off the old Hugh Smith block: precise, cheerful, business-like and not very much more.' Margot was Asquith's wife, but their marriage had broken down. Quite what Lancy was doing with the Prime Minister's wife is not spelled out. As she was a member of the wealthy Tennant family, he probably looked after her investments and, in this situation, was no more than her 'walker'.

These various calls to arms left George Rowe, Fred Pitman and Malcolm Pilkington to run a much-reduced firm. So long as the Stock Exchange was officially closed for local business between September 1914 and January 1915, the salaries of all staff were cut by 20 per cent. Single men at the front received no extra pay to supplement their incomes. However all married men had their service allowance made up to 80 per cent of their salaries, and a clerk whose mother was a widow was treated as a married man. In all some thirty partners and staff served during the war, three of whom did not return – Julian Biddell, John Birmington and Julian Martin Smith.

In the crisis situation of the first year of the war, commission income dropped to £24,395, lower than in 1901. However it picked up significantly in 1915 after Rowe & Pitman (befitting perhaps from its new 'official' status) became the beneficiary of a decree that conscripted all British assets in the United States so that the government could borrow against them in New York. When the Bank of England (or its agent, J.P. Morgan) needed to realize any holdings it usually used Rowe & Pitman – a source of profitable business. In addition, the firm could still rely on some regular flows of income, particularly from Malcolm Pilkington's contacts in the insurance industry. (While commissions were increasing again this way, general expenses had fallen by a third – the result of the reduced payroll.)

The war brought its own problems and opportunities. There was the question of what to do about clients with open trades who were now serving in France – the cause of a dispute with jobbers Harris Winthrop. And in the general xenophobia, German-born stockbrokers were no longer allowed to practise. One such firm, Nelke Phillips, reacted by selling out to Vickers da Costa. Inevitably, with this competition removed, Rowe & Pitman was able to garner new business.

Nevertheless there was much work for Lancy to do when he returned from the war. Although technically Senior Partner only

After the War

towards the end of his life (since Fred Pitman, the founder, remained with the firm until 1940), Lancy was definitely the driving force in the firm. Both Rowe and Watson were now reaching retirement age. Watson's brother had left the Scottish Provident, so that source of business had practically dried up. Lancy's ideas and contacts were needed more than ever.

He first turned to the 'family bank'. Until recently, of course, this had been Smith's Bank. But this long-established institution had failed to weather the economic storms of the 1890s and had been absorbed by the Union Bank of London (later to become part of the National Westminster Bank group). Lancy's mother, Constance, was most discomfited by the family's 'failure to hold their own in the onward march of banking interests'. She wrote:

> In 1902 a great blow fell upon the Smith family in the sudden announcement that the old established bank of Smith, Payne & Smith was to be amalgamated with the Union Bank of London. It fell like a thunderclap upon Hugh, to whom nothing had been said – not even by his own nephew Gerald – nor has been to this day, which has wounded him deeply.... I never felt more angry, and the feeling was shared by all our sons.

C.J. Hambro and Son had survived this early Edwardian clear-out of banks. But, as with many other financial institutions, the war had taken its toll. In 1920 it still had funds tied up in German and Austrian debts which its six partners were forced to carry themselves. So when that year it was approached by its close associate, the British Bank of Northern Commerce (BBNC) with a view to a merger, it jumped at the opportunity. Initially the new bank was called Hambros Bank of Northern Commerce (with offices at BBNC's former building in 41 and 43 Bishopsgate), but this name was considered too unwieldy and was abbreviated to Hambros Bank in 1921. The following year Lancy arranged for Rowe & Pitman to rent – albeit temporarily – the fourth and fifth floors at 43 Bishopsgate, above the new Hambros Bank. Although the adoption of the firm as Hambros' regular broker had to await the death of Sir Everard Hambro in 1935, the stage was set for a new phase in Rowe & Pitman's history.

Lancy found that the city had changed dramatically as a result of the war. Most obviously London was no longer the centre of the financial world. The dollar had overtaken the pound as the currency for international trade and sovereign issues. German and Central European debt continued to weigh down the banking system until the acceptance of the Dawes Plan in 1924. Overall, this created an atavistic feeling that Britain only needed to return to the gold standard and all would be well. But when that happened in 1925 it was a disaster, pegging the still-floundering British economy to an overvalued exchange rate.

Lancy orientated Rowe & Pitman to take advantage of any business possibilities it could. In international loans the firm hung onto the coat-tails of J.S. Morgan, the biggest player in the New York market. There was a flurry of important company issues in Britain. The growing democratization of the markets led to a demand for new investment trusts in London. The Scottish Provident might no longer be a great source of business, but Rowe & Pitman now had links with Thomson McLintock, a leading firm of Scottish chartered accountants, which not only became its auditors, but also established the Grange Investment Trust, in which Rowe & Pitman played an important management role. At the same time, the bulk of the country's wealth was still tied up in the land. So Lancy worked hard to attract wealthy members of the British aristocracy to Rowe & Pitman's client list.

Competition between brokers was fierce as they tried to claw back business. In April 1922, Rowe & Pitman saw fit to complain to the Stock Exchange that Mullens, the government broker, was trying to poach one of its established clients, Christ Church, Oxford. These unique circumstances arose out of a circular from the Ministry of Agriculture enjoining university colleagues to move from short into longer-dated securities, and recommending its own broker, Mullens, to advise on the matter. Apprised of Rowe & Pitman's concern, the Ministry replied that, under the Universities and College Estates Acts, it held 'securities to a considerable amount on behalf of certain Universities and

After the War

Colleges and that all transactions in relation to such securities are carried out by the Ministry through their brokers, Messers Mullens Marshall Steer Lawford and Co.'

Proximity to Hambros brought rewards as Rowe & Pitman moved sharply to grab a share of the post-war new issue market. Lancy's wartime job as Chairman of the Tobacco and Matches Control Board put the firm in line for several successful issues in the 1920s, including Bryant & May and Gallahers. Rowe & Pitman's Scandinavian connections made it doubly appropriate for it, in conjunction with Laing & Cruikshank, to float several issues for the Swedish Match Company owned by Ivar Kreuger, who at one time was responsible for 75 per cent of the matches produced in the world. Debentures in the 'Swedish Match King's' personal vehicle, Kreuger & Toll, were highly successful, bringing good profits to Rowe & Pitman clients. His business empire turned out to have been built on matchsticks, however, and he committed suicide, as his companies failed around him, in March 1932.

Another of Lancy's wartime jobs – on the Admiralty's Interdepartmental Oil Committee – stimulated his interest in the oil business. He became friends with the two leading oil magnates of the day, Sir Henri Deterding of the Royal Dutch Petroleum Company and Walter Bearstead, who ran the family trading-group-cum-finance-house which his father Marcus had built into the Shell Oil Company, before selling out to Deterding. Lancy was delighted when Bearstead used Rowe & Pitman to make a £2 million swap on the gilt-edged market: he did the deal himself, describing it 'as easy as dealing in a 500 share market'. Deterding he simply called the most interesting client the firm ever had.

High on Lancy's list of priorities was building up a new set of principals. He had never been particularly enthusiastic about the appointment of Walter White, the money market man who had become a full partner in 1917. More to his taste was 'Jock' Bowes-Lyon, the Eton and New College, Oxford educated son of the fourteenth Earl of Strathmore, who joined the firm in 1919 and became a sharing partner three years later. Bowes-Lyon, whose sister was to be the wife of King George VI, had been badly injured on the Western Front in 1916. Although much liked by his colleagues, his active participation in the City was minimal. But, prior to his tragically early death in February 1930 at the age of forty-three, he did his duty in attracting what today would be called 'high net worth individuals' among his relatives and friends.

Close to home, Bowes-Lyon arranged for his sister Elizabeth's marriage settlement with Prince Bertie, then Duke of York, later to be King George VI, to be administered by Rowe & Pitman. Thus was established a long-standing relationship with the woman who was to become Queen Elizabeth the Queen Mother. In later years a myth arose that Rowe & Pitman were stockbrokers to the British royal family. However this was the preserve of James Capel, with Rowe & Pitman's role limited to executing occasional orders on behalf of Coutts, the royal bankers.

Rowe & Pitman contented itself with acting for a cross-section of international royalty, including the Kings of Greece and Spain, the Shah of Persia and Prince Paul of Serbia, who was a regular visitor to Bishopsgate. The firm also had many wealthy British aristocrats as clients. The Dukes of Westminster, perhaps the richest of them all, used Rowe & Pitman. When the list of investments owned by Bend'or, the second Duke, was printed, it ran to twenty-eight pages. He required Rowe & Pitman to value his holdings every month and to send a report to his solicitors Boodle Hatfield. Taking on the Duke meant having to advise his mistresses. Harold Wimpress, a clerk in the Private Clients Department, became adept at knowing which woman was in favour, and which not.

The Dukes of Marlborough also engaged Rowe & Pitman's services. But the tenth Duke's custom was lost when he telephoned the office, shortly after the Second World War, and spoke to a young trainee. When the man at the other end of the line announced he was the Duke of Marlborough, the whipper-snapper replied, 'Oh yes, and I'm the Queen of Sheba.'

By then the heyday of the private client had passed. But for three decades at the start of the century, Rowe & Pitman was

After the War

arguably the leading private client broker. Customers ranged from Apsley Cherry-Garrard, the Antarctic explorer who wrote the classic travel book, *The Worst Journey in the World*, to Agatha Christie, the hugely successful crime novelist.

Lancy was particularly adept at winning the confidence of rich industrialists and financiers, from Lord Beaverbrook, the newspaper baron, and Sir Henri Deterding, the oil magnate (of both of whom more later), to Sir David Yule, the son of an Edinburgh Writer to the Signet who made a fortune running his uncle's firm, the Calcutta trading house Andrew Yule and Company. After this business was sold to Morgan Grenfell in 1916, Sir David took a room in its agent's office, Yule, Catto and Company. Lancy used to visit him every morning, and even he was wont to tip his hat to Sir David who, as well as joining the boards of Vickers, Royal Exchange Assurance and Midland Bank, 'did business on a very big scale'. One happy memory was his acquisition of a single tranche of 20,000 Hambros Bank shares through Rowe & Pitman. The man also 'had charm beyond belief', according to Lancy, who acted for the estate when Sir David died in 1928, worth £13 million.

More down to earth than Bowes-Lyon, and a huge asset to Rowe & Pitman, was Fred Pitman's 30-year-old nephew, Hugo, who became a partner in March 1922, on the very day George Rowe formally retired. Not that this young man was a slouch when it came to introducing well-connected clients: the word in the office was that Hugo Pitman, another product of Eton and New College, got the job on the strength of a luncheon interview with Lancy, during which he had the good sense to mention that he had dined with Lady Strathclyde the previous evening.

Hugo Pitman followed in the family tradition of rowing. He was one of the successful Oxford University Boat Race crew in 1912, and in the same year he also won an Olympic silver medal. Burdened with a war-time injury which left him deaf (particularly at awkward moments when it suited him), he was the only man who rivalled Lancy – initially in his intellect and range of accomplishments, later in his professionalism and the number of his clients. Married to a niece of the American painter John

Sargent, he was passionately interested in the arts. An excellent draftsman and artist in his own right, he was an important collector of modern paintings. Madame Suggia, the well-known cellist, was a close friend, as was Augustus John, to whom he acted as a financial adviser. In his later years he was a Trustee of the Tate Gallery.

After two years, another new partner arrived, sporting family connections. Fitzjames Graham Watson, a 32-year-old Old Etonian, was the nephew of the recently departed Guthrie Watson, with all his Cunliffe kinship. While he never had his uncle's entrée to Charlotte Square, 'Fitz', as he was known, was to play an important role in the professionalization (again that word) of Rowe & Pitman's links with City of London. A new generation of unit and investment trusts was emerging, while the old merchant banks and insurance companies were as eager to do business as ever. Alive to the opportunities, Fitz was to develop such a close and easy relationship with Hambros, the bank down below, that he regularly attended its board meetings.

A third post-war partner came because of Lancy's new-found interest in the oil business. Having read the book, *The Oil Trust and Anglo-American Relations* in the mid-1920s, he was impressed enough to approach its two authors, Sydney Russell Cooke and Nicholas Davenport for further enlightenment. When Cooke turned out to be a stockbroker in the respected firm Capel-Cure & Terry, Lancy invited him to join Rowe & Pitman. Cooke insisted on bringing his co-author with him. So in October 1925 Cooke became a partner, while Davenport was hired as a clerk to start up a long-overdue market intelligence section. (For some reason Cooke's appointment was prominently displayed in *The Times*, which led the Stock Exchange to enquire if Rowe & Pitman had been advertising. George Rowe, in his retirement, was hauled before the Exchange's General Purposes Committee to explain that the announcement had been sent to *The Times* in the ordinary way and the firm played no role in determining its position in the paper.)

Cooke and Davenport, by then in their early thirties, had been at school at Cheltenham together. While the former went to

After the War

Cambridge and the latter to Oxford, they linked up after the war as part of a group of economists loosely attached to the 'architect of the peace', J.M. Keynes. As stockbrokers, they took very different approaches. Cooke adapted easily to life at 43 Bishopsgate, while Davenport remained at heart a left-leaning journalist who could not conceal his distaste for the old-boy network of finance and privilege which revolved around Lancy. Not so obvious was Cooke's slant on the world. For, like several people associated with Rowe & Pitman, he was a spy, who ended the First World War attached to MI5, certainly continuing this career into the 1920s.

When, in September 1928, Virginia Woolf met Cooke and his wife at a dinner party also attended by Keynes, she was not impressed by this prototype James Bond. She found him 'a bounder, a climber, a shoving young man, who wants to be smart, cultivated, go ahead and all the rest of it'. (Interestingly Mrs Cooke, known as 'Melville', was the daughter of Captain E.J. Smith, master of the ill-fated liner, the *Titanic*, which had sunk in the Atlantic in April 1912, with the loss of 1,503 lives and a number of Rowe & Pitman American share certificates for which Lloyd's later issued indemnity letters.)

It was as a spy rather than as a stockbroker that Cooke took a close interest in the young Soviet Union, and this seems to have led to his premature death in 1930. Many of his relatives and friends were prominent figures in the intelligence world. His sister was married to the brother of Brigadier Arthur Harker, deputy head of MI5. Best man at his wedding was Sir Campbell Stuart, Deputy Director of Propaganda in Enemy Countries throughout the First World War.

Later Cooke was encouraged to maintain contacts with leading Bolsheviks. Trotsky's brother-in-law, Leo Kamenev, a prominent Politburo member who was shot on Stalin's orders in 1937, was invited to visit Cooke's family house in the Isle of Wight in August 1920, when he was in London as part of a trade mission. He came with Winston Churchill's cousin, the artist Clare Sheridan, who had sculpted his bust in London. What is now clear is that Cooke was Sheridan's MI5 'control', using her to obtain intelligence about closed circles in the Soviet Union. Having encouraged her in her determination to visit Moscow to make further sculptures of Bolsheviks the following month, he was the last person she saw before travelling to Russia, via Stockholm. With his own links to espionage and to the Baltic, Lancy probably encouraged his new protégé to stay close to this secret world.

A decade later, in July 1930, the 37-year-old Cooke was found dead, with a double-barrelled sporting gun lying nearby, in a flat in King's Bench Walk Temple, which he rented from his friend Nicholas Davenport. An inquest recorded that Cooke had shot himself accidentally while cleaning his gun, but rumours of Soviet involvement persisted. Hugo Pitman, who was not a great fabricator of tales, told a young colleague specifically that Cooke had been shot by the Russians.

Davenport led a rather more humdrum existence. He laid the foundations for the research department which became an important ingredient in Rowe & Pitman's success in later years. But when he was refused a partnership, he left for another broker. Towards the end of his life, after a distinguished career as an economist, he published *Memoirs of a City Radical*, which was scathing about his time at Rowe & Pitman. 'I found myself in a snobbish upper-class firm,' he wrote uncompromisingly.

> Lancelot Hugh Smith, the head of Rowe & Pitman, had royalty among his friends, his clients and even his relations. He was the father figure of the great Hugh Smith clan which had brothers, nephews and cousins entrenched in the merchant banks, investment trusts and other financial institutions throughout the city.
>
> For me, Lancy stood for the Establishment, as I had imagined it to be – pompous, powerful, upright, unbending, alert to defend the pound sterling to the last million of the reserves, and to the last million of the wretched unemployed. All the immense Stock Exchange business of the Hugh Smith clan poured through Rowe & Pitman. In addition to this bread and butter the firm floated many company issues and handed out underwriting to the life insurance companies and banks whose business it handled.

After the War

The profits of the firm were therefore enormous. The Partners enjoyed fabulous incomes. Naturally they lived in great style with town and country houses, and many of them hunted in the shires. Sidney Russell Cooke and his wife Melville hunted with the Pytchley and looked magnificent on their splendid mounts.

The year after Cooke and Davenport joined the firm, the stalwart Malcolm Pilkington died at the surprisingly young age of fifty-two. Lancy turned to Andrew Vanneck, whom he poached from the stock department of Lazards. Vanneck, a nephew of the fourth Baron Huntingfield, had served in the Scots Guards with Hugh Kindersley, later Chairman of Lazards. A hard-working stockbroker of the old school, he was close to English Electric (later GEC), where Rowe & Pitman was itching to become brokers, and he had useful contacts in the oil business, particularly with Shell. He also had a fierce temper. After a row with a partner, he refused to speak to him, insisting on using a clerk to communicate. Bert Williamson, an office messenger, lived to tell how Vanneck hurled a Cardex box at him, splintering the door behind him, because he had produced Lord Saumarez's folder instead of Lord Somers's.

Some years later, in November 1935, Vanneck caused the firm some embarrassment when both he and Rowe & Pitman, acting for Hambros Bank, were severely censured by the Stock Exchange for failing to release enough shares in a new issue for Thos Firth and John Brown Ltd. Vanneck explained that Hambros had wanted to establish an orderly market in the shares. But Rowe & Pitman's long-established jobbers, now calling themselves Kitchin Baker Mason, said there were simply not enough shares to make a market. The Stock Exchange brought a charge under Clause 1 of its draconian Rule 17. Since this implied some dishonesty, Rowe & Pitman protested vigorously. Later however Fred Pitman admitted that Vanneck had 'made a grave mistake in not seeing that the initial block available for the market was inadequate'.

The only other partner to join in the 1920s was Fred Chitty, an expert in gilt-edged stocks, who replaced Walter White in the discount market when the latter retired in March 1928. In some respects Chitty was a throw-back to the old days when rowing was the way into the firm (his kinsman, Sir Joseph Chitty, was a well-known lawyer who for a long time had acted as umpire of the University Boat race). He himself enjoys an important place in the history of high finance, however, as the man who introduced Siegmund Warburg into the City.

Perhaps the client who summed up the range and the flavour of Rowe & Pitman's (and particularly Lancy's) dealings in the 1920s was Max Aitken, the Canadian financier and newspaper owner who was created Lord Beaverbrook in 1916, in recognition of his war-time political and propaganda activity. It was a business relationship based on friendship and propriety. In May 1923, for example, Lancy took the trouble to write to Beaverbrook sympathizing about the latter's friend, Andrew Bonar Law, who had been forced to resign as Prime Minister through ill health. A few days later he sent him a copy of the third volume of William Hickey's *Diaries*, which clearly had some significance. Beaverbrook had acquired the *Daily Express* in 1916, and Lancy may well have been responsible for suggesting Hickey's name for the newspaper's well-known social diary column. (A recent Beaverbrook biography suggested that the name was plucked at random from the Dictionary of National Biography, which is clearly wrong.)

The following year, Lancy wrote to Beaverbrook, asking if he could sit next to Mrs Grenville at his banquet the following week. 'If I can get away Friday I'll come and play tennis with you,' he added. Beaverbrook, typically, did not allow Lancy his wish, telling his friend, 'I have placed you next to the prettiest woman in Canada – the wife of Frank Jones, the general manager of the Cement Company. On your left is a very pretty American girl.'

In this atmosphere Lancy felt relaxed enough to ask business favours of his friend. His brother Vivian had been appointed a governor of the Royal Exchange Assurance Corporation and Lancy was looking to this institution to provide Rowe & Pitman with the sort of business that used to come from the Scottish

Provident. In November 1923, after Beaverbrook had bought the *Evening Standard* from Sir Edward Hulton, Lancy wrote with what might have seemed a trifling request:

> Might I venture to remind you about the Royal Exchange Assurance Corporation's insurance in Manchester which they hold from the Hulton Companies. I am exceedingly close to the Royal Exchange in every way, and if you could use any influence to prevent any possibility of this insurance being removed from them owing to the change in ownership of the Hulton Press, I should be more than grateful.

He returned the favour by giving employment to Beaverbrook's wayward young friend Viscount Castlerosse. All things being equal, Castlerosse might have been cut out for a career in the City, since his uncle was Lord Revelstoke, head of Baring's. But his lordship was not suited to stockbroking: his most memorable contribution to Rowe & Pitman was the specially reinforced sofa which had to be acquired to accommodate him and his postprandial siestas in the office. Lancy used to say that Castlerosse 'would not cross the road to do a day's work', and was quite happy to let him go so that he could pursue a career in journalism. Subsequently Lancy's main concern was to ensure that the young man did not fall too far into debt. When Castlerosse was landed with a £20,000 obligation that arose from buying stocks on margin, Lancy took a particular interest in seeing that Beaverbrook paid the sum off.

Today Lancy might be accused of running an insider dealers' club. In November 1930, for example, he and Beaverbrook entered a long debate about the future of Deterding's most widely quoted Shell Union shares. 'The Beaver' was clearly convinced the price of the stock was about to fall. But Lancy, after consulting his friend Sir Henri, begged to differ. Not quite a year later Beaverbrook wrote to Lancy once more with the news that he had 'some American money. What do you say to Shell Union, at present price.... I am quite content to follow Sir

Henri Deterding if he is satisfied. And I have done so for some time.' Lancy replied that since Deterding was away, he could not be sure; he felt the oil business was bad and could go lower. Two months later he contacted Beaverbrook again, with the news that Deterding had returned from an extended gout cure on the continent and was bullish about his oil shares.

In between times there was serious business to be conducted. On 10 May 1923, for example, we find Lancy sending Beaverbrook 'all the particulars of the USA Dutch East Indies dollar loans'. The Canadian magnate did not appear interested, for the next day he replied that he thought he would 'wait for your new issues and avail myself of some new underwriting if you give me the offer'.

The following year, Beaverbrook asked him to recommend a modest but high-yielding investment for a young relative. Lancy's detailed reply on 23 May was revealing: 'I received a message from you asking for suggestions for the investment of £1,500 in securities to yield 10%, the amount of each security to be limited to £500. This is not easy. However, I can but do my best.' Lancy took pains to list his recommendations, which included De Beers 40 per cent £2 10s 0d Cumulative Preference Shares at 11½, yield £8 19s 3d; Swedish Matches 100 Swedish Kroner Shares (with an autograph note from Lancy: 'These shares will improve'); Central Mining and Investment Corporation £8 Shares at 10½; and Roneo Limited 10% Cumulative Preference Shares of £1. 'Of these suggestions I prefer the Swedish Matches and the Central Mining, in which I have the very greatest confidence,' said Lancy, 'and next I take the De Beers Pref. The De Beers have defaulted in the past, but all arrears have been paid up.'

Lancy's dealings with Beaverbrook highlight Rowe & Pitman's growing liaison with two City institutions, Schroders and Helbert Wagg. By the mid-1920s investment trusts and syndicates were much in vogue. In May 1924 Rowe & Pitman sent Beaverbrook a circular on the Continental Commercial Trust, for which £500,000 was being raised. 'The Company is being formed under the auspices of Messrs J.H. Schroder and of

Baron Bruno Schroder in particular. The object of the formation is that the Company's funds should be invested in industrial, banking, shipping and other undertakings in Central Europe, and particularly in Germany.' Beaverbrook immediately counted himself in for 500 shares at £10 each.

Later that year Beaverbrook had clearly asked Lancy's advice on an article being produced for one of his newspapers on the London Stock market. Lancy later revealed that the source of his information on jobbers was 'my friend Wagg', or Alfred Wagg, son of the stockbroker who in 1900 had been so unimpressive with his command of detail about the Camp Bird mine in Colorado.

By the 1920s Helbert Wagg had changed its line of business. It had abandoned stockbroking and become an issuing house, working closely with Rowe & Pitman. (On complicated issues, Helbert Wagg looked to Schroders – a relationship which was to result in the merger of the two firms nearly forty years later.) As was the case with Beaverbrook and so many others, Lancy's dealings with Alfred Wagg were based on a personal friendship. This had arisen from a shared interest in the Eton Manor Boys' Club in East London. Lancy became a supporter in memory of his cousin Julian Martin Smith, who had run the club gym.

For all his airs and graces, Lancy knew how to sell a stock when required. In March 1925 he sent Beaverbrook details of a 'special arrangement' regarding the Continental Baking Corporation whose 8% Preferred Stock was to be offered in New York later that week. '[We are] in a position to offer you 1000 shares at $100 each,' Lancy told Beaverbrook, 'with a bonus in B Common Shares at the rate of 35 B shares per 100 Preferred Shares.' He added that an accompanying memo from Helbert Wagg explained that B shares currently stood at $28 in the New York market. However, 'We have to request that you will keep this offer of B stock absolutely confidential, as no such bonus will be given in connection with the marketing of the Preferred Shares in New York.'

Around this time Rowe & Pitman began producing its own

printed marketing tools – a monthly *Oil Report* and *Securities for Investment* circular. Beaverbrook was impressed; in October 1927 he wrote to congratulate Lancy on these publications, which he described as 'first-rate material extraordinarily well used'. If Lancy thought that Beaverbrook knew anything about the subject of the *Securities for Investment* circular, he sent him a proof for comment. Thus, when he received an advance copy of the circular on Canadian Newsprint Shares in September 1928, Beaverbrook wrote back to say he would 'not recommend shares of Canada Power and Paper at this present time' but thought that Rowe & Pitman 'should recommend shares of International Paper'.

Rowe & Pitman did not always jump to Beaverbrook's demands. In November 1929, for example, he wanted the firm to raise money for the Calgary Power Company, but it proved unable to do so. A couple of months earlier an unfortunate failing in the Rowe & Pitman clerical department came to light when a Beaverbrook minion was forced to write testily to the firm, 'I regret that it is necessary to draw your attention again to the correct address to which all communications to Lord Beaverbrook should be sent. You will observe that the enclosed envelope has been addressed to Garden Court, which offices we vacated in 1925.'

As Beaverbrook increasingly acted as a press magnate, he used Rowe & Pitman to build up his stakes in newspaper companies. Towards the end of the 1920s the firm was regularly in the market buying and selling shares in the London Express and Daily Mail Trust companies, often using nominee names. At one time Beaverbrook was the second largest shareholder in his rival Lord Rothermere's Daily Mail Trust, until Lancy arranged the sale of these shares for a consideration which netted Beaverbrook £500,000.

Lancy was not above benefiting personally from this connection. On one occasion Beaverbrook offered him 100 shares in a new issue of Evening Standard 8% Preference Shares. When Lancy accepted, his friend told him, 'I suppose all the shares belong to you, and they are simply put in other names for convenience. The shares are valuable ones.' Such practices, although widespread at the time, would clearly be frowned on today.

4   The Camp Bird

LANCY WAS A MAN of many talents, but painting was not generally considered one of them. That did not deter him from taking up his brushes (shades of his friend Winston Churchill, perhaps) and executing a couple of watercolours, which for a long time hung close together in the Bishopsgate office. One portrayed a magnificent *rara avis* which was labelled 'The Camp Bird', the other the same creature with ruffled plumage, surrounded by a team of disgruntled speculators. The pictures were painted by Lancy after the temporary failure of the Camp Bird Mine in 1920. Originally started in 1900, it had provided high returns for two decades until suddenly it stopped paying dividends. Lancy's artistic efforts symbolized the uncertain mood of the early 1930s.

The previous few years had been buoyant, as Rowe & Pitman capitalized on the new issues boom of the late 1920s. The firm's outstanding success was the flotation of Ford Motors, an early exercise in what today would be called corporate finance. Rowe & Pitman's involvement resulted from Hugo Pitman's friendship with Henry Ford, heir to the multinational motor-car company. As a result, Rowe & Pitman was chosen as Ford Motors' lead broker when the US firm needed to raise money on the London market in December 1928. Ford's particular objective was to finance a new 300-acre factory at Dagenham, which was described as the largest in the world. With Morgan Grenfell as the issuing house, Rowe & Pitman obtained a preferential allotment of 900,000 out of a total 2.8 million Ford shares, out of which it had to supply clients, friends and partners, even Lancy's barber. With Americans piling into the market, everyone looked on happily as the shares climbed to a £1 premium on day one of trading, then £3 on day two, eventually climbing to around £5. Apart from these profits, Rowe & Pitman received a fee of £2,000 for obtaining leave to deal, with an additional allotment commission of 1½d per share.

As a result net profits topped £200,000 for the first time in 1928/29 – well over double the £78,000 recorded only seven years previously. This volume of business required an increasingly professional service from the 'back office'. Here Harry Little, the Wrangler who had joined in 1900, was in overall charge. Although he had started on the minimal salary of £55, his qualities were quickly recognized, and by 1914 he was earning £550. Little was assisted by Bill Palmer, another Old Olavian, who had taken over the more mundane duties of Office Manager when Tommy Britton died in the mid-1920s. Under them 'Gertie' Miller, yet another product of St Olave's, had followed Little as the indispensable clerk in the crucial American Department.

Together they devised an in-house system for recording allotments, commissions and dividends – particularly useful when there was large demand for a stock. The system broke down when one issue was so popular that Rowe & Pitman ran out of application forms. At the time newspapers only published application forms on the day of flotation. On this occasion, Little sent one of the office boys out to purchase 1,000 copies of the *Daily Express*. At crack of dawn, he set the staff to work with scissors and pens. They attacked the newspapers and eventually completed the requisite number of applications before the lists closed.

The interpretation of the official rules regarding commissions sometimes caused problems. Prior to the First World War stockbrokers had charged what they liked as commission, and they were usually very competitive. But in 1912 the Stock Exchange introduced a scale with a minimum commission. This endured for nearly fifty years until 1961, despite initial opposition from the larger stockbrokers, including Rowe & Pitman, which fought to liberalize the rules and, in particular, to lower the minimum commission. Difficulties tended to arise over the meaning of the 'best terms' clause, while back in the old days, Wilfred White, the gilts partner, used to antagonize clients by neglecting to tell them that full commission was chargeable on the first £2,500 worth of any deal.

More uncertain days were heralded by the collapse of Clarence Hatry's industrial and financial empire in 1929. The specific cause of this débâcle was Hatry's ambitious attempt to restructure the British steel industry with the help of fraudulently issued share certificates. Although the general public was badly hit in the £14 million swindle, the Stock Exchange insisted that all bargains should be honoured. To this end it appointed Fred Pitman (still nominally a partner until 1940) to chair a committee which would arrange all settlements. Although it was not badly affected itself, Rowe & Pitman contributed £1,000 to a fund (eventually totalling £1 million) which helped to ensure that anyone who wanted to sell his Hatry shares received payment. The firm also provided the services of Harry Little to head the team in charge of the nuts and bolts of the settlement. As a token of its gratitude, the Stock Exchange Council presented Rowe & Pitman with a handsome pair of strawberry dishes made by Charles Martin of London in 1758. Mounted on wooden stands, they were inscribed 'Presented to the Partners of Rowe & Pitman by fellow members of the Stock Exchange as a small token of gratitude for great services rendered in connection with the settlement of the serious financial crisis September 1929-February 1930.'

Hatry's failure was followed by the Wall Street crash a few weeks later, and the dark days of economic recession, which culminated in Britain's painful ditching of the gold standard in September 1931. During that year, new issues ground to a halt (Cazenove's, with five issues, led the league table of brokers), and Rowe & Pitman's profits halved to little over £82,000.

The 1930s brought a mood of retrenchment to Rowe & Pitman's offices. Staff numbers and wages were pegged back. Even the partners had to make sacrifices, as Lancy ordered them to forgo port with their lunch, unless a visitor was present. Lancy himself adopted an increasingly paternalistic role (not always viewed as benevolent by his staff). A feature of the firm's calendar became the annual outing to The Old Hall, the mansion in Garboldisham, Norfolk, where he now spent much of his time. He still retained both his share of Mount Clare, the Smith seat in Roehampton, and his house in Charles Street, Mayfair. But Garboldisham, with its rolling shoots and proximity to the royal family at Sandringham, allowed him to entertain in the style he wanted.

If anything, Lancy became more of a caricature of himself – which gave rise to a perhaps apocryphal story. A duke and a business tycoon died within a short time of one another and their memorial services were arranged for the same day. This left Lancy with something of a dilemma. After discussing the matter with Bill Palmer, who looked after his personal affairs, he attended the tycoon's service, having decided that it would attract more dukes than the peer's.

During the pre-war decade five new partners were recruited. The first, Simon Rodney, came shortly after Jock Bowes-Lyon's untimely death in 1930. Son of the seventh Baron Rodney and husband of the daughter of the first Viscount Greenwood, he had the sort of family connections to please Lancy. More importantly in the climate of the time, he brought useful business relationships, particularly a link with the steel-making Keen family. Previously Cazenove had dominated steel issues, but Rowe & Pitman's new-found liaison with Guest, Keen & Nettlefold helped it later become an important force in this area of industrial finance. While developing into a first-rate stockbroker, Rodney never took the City too seriously. When one of his generally Old Etonian fellow partners referred to 'm'tutors', he, as a product of Rugby, would ask for the stock's price, as though they had been referring to one of the firm's investment tips, like the N'Changa copper mine in Central Africa.

Arthur Anderson was already working for Laurence Sons and Gardner when Lancy sought his advice about a potential recruit. The 44-year-old Anderson, a traditional product of Eton and Trinity College, Cambridge, suggested that he could do the job rather better himself. A powerful force in the 1950s, when he became Senior Partner, Anderson helped perpetuate Rowe & Pitman's excellent boardroom connections in Edinburgh, where his father was a partner in the leading solicitor, J. and F. Anderson. (A Pitman cousin also worked there.) Once a top sprinter, who represented Britain at the 1912 Olympic Games in Stockholm, Anderson is remembered for his gnomic utterances, which combined equal parts of naïvety and menace. Since talking shop was not allowed in the partners' dining room, he would regale unsuspecting investment managers with gratuitous information about the number of wing beats a heron makes to the minute or how the Queen Mary's maximum speed was geared to the square root of its waterline length. Sometimes he would surprise these essentially urban creatures with questions like 'Do you still use the neck shot for stags?' His coded way of inquiring if a man wanted to visit the lavatory, 'Are you clean?', caused one guest to stammer in reply, 'No, I'm Walker of the Royal.' And he had his own inimitable way of putting an end to a meal. 'Now I must go and tighten my stays,' he would announce.

As a bachelor Lancy had no children, but he kept the Smith flame alive by appointing two of his nephews to the partnership in the late 1930s. Hughie Smith was the son of Lancy's eldest brother Vivian, of Morgan Grenfell. A product of Eton and Oxford, he was still only twenty-four when he joined in 1935, shortly after marrying the daughter of the sixth Earl of Rosebery. Esmond Baring was a year younger in 1937. He was the son of Lancy's sister Olive and Guy Baring, the second son of Lord Ashburton (a Baring family title). Guy Baring had been killed in action with the Coldstream Guards in 1916. After Eton and Trinity College, Cambridge, Esmond spent a year learning the ropes of the City with Baring Brothers before joining his cousin Hughie at Rowe & Pitman.

In between these two came the man who, outside the City, is the best-known Rowe & Pitman partner of all. In 1935, when he joined the firm on the recommendation of Hughie Vivian Smith, a golfing acquaintance, Ian Fleming had done very little with his life. Aged twenty-seven, he had tried and failed to be an army officer, diplomat, journalist and banker. One of his partners at Rowe & Pitman called him 'the world's worst stockbroker'.

Fleming was considered potentially useful because his grandfather had started the powerful Robert Fleming bank, where his uncle was Chairman. As Lancy observed around this time, 'I always felt that if they keep their heads up and their overheads down, a firm containing three members of great City families [Smith, Fleming and Baring] must succeed.' In Fleming's case this connection yielded very little. The dashing young Old Etonian delighted in recommending risky stocks in out of the way places, and is remembered for having only one regular client. The literary talent which later led him to compose the hugely successful James Bond novels was put to work on the first ever Rowe & Pitman corporate history. However Lancy did not like the finished product (he thought it emphasized the Pitman connection too much) and consigned this early Fleming *œuvre* to the waste-paper basket. Fleming then occupied himself with writing Rowe & Pitman's *Securities for Investment* circulars.

Fleming's main asset was his considerable personal charm. He struck up a warm friendship with Hugo Pitman, who insisted on taking him on a business trip to the United States in October 1937. Fleming distinguished himself by leaving an important dinner saying he was unwell. Returning later to his hotel Pitman looked into Fleming's room to see if his condition had improved and found the young man propped up in bed with a glass of whisky and a blonde. Through Pitman, Fleming met members of the Morgan family, who proved helpful when he next returned as Personal Assistant to the Director of Naval Intelligence in 1941. The Rowe & Pitman connection with the intelligence services was perpetuated – not surprisingly perhaps since Lancy's brother Aubrey was one of the men who interviewed Fleming for the job.

Hilary Bray, a friend of Fleming's who joined the partnership after the Second World War, observed much later:

> Ian wouldn't have a chance now of getting away with life at Rowe & Pitman as he did in the days when he was there. He was

From Diamond Sculls to Golden Handcuffs

accepted on the old boy basis because of his connections with Robert Fleming. Nowadays he would have to learn a great deal of Stock Exchange law and the techniques of finance, but then he was virtually able to write his own part.

Of more lasting value to the firm was the recruitment of a young clerk, Bill Corney, in 1936. He was another St Olave's alumnus, who had graduated from Imperial College, London, with a degree in mathematics. After a short-lived job plotting weapons' trajectories at the Woolwich Arsenal, he applied to join what had often been referred to as the school workfare system at Rowe & Pitman. He was interviewed by Harry Little and Bill Palmer, who told him regretfully that the partners had banned the recruitment of anyone else from their school because it was creating an office hierarchy which led to considerable resentment. Little's own son, Arthur, had been prevented from joining Rowe & Pitman for this reason and was working unhappily as a jobber.

However, the firm needed someone with Corney's numeracy skills. So, by special dispensation, he joined as a clerk in the statistical department, which at the time was run by Nicholas Davenport's successor, a gold expert called Lawrence Wilkinson who, after joining Beaverbrook's Express Newspapers, became so obsessed with this commodity that it drove him mad. Corney's starting pay was £187 a year, though he was denied the additional bonus he had been promised because of an economic slump.

Within a short time the partners came to rely on Corney's head for figures combined, uniquely, with a deep understanding of Stock Exchange law. This did not always mean the principals took his advice, however. On one occasion Corney put up a list of suggestions to 'Uncle Arthur' Anderson in the latter's capacity as a trustee of the W.P. Tyzer estate. Under the 1925 Trustee Act, which was in force at the time, Australia 5% 1955 was considered to be a trustee investment when it could be bought for less than its redemption price, but non-trustee when over par. Afterwards, checking the contract sheet, Corney was horrified to

The Camp Bird

see that Anderson and his fellow trustees had bought Australia 5% at over par. But when he pointed this out, Anderson looked at him coldly and said, 'Corney, one thing you must learn is that it doesn't matter whether you think a stock is a trustee stock or not. I think Australia 5% is a trustee stock and that's the end of the matter.'

During the late 1930s the numbers of staff had grown again and had reached around a hundred. In the general relaxation, Lancy discovered that the partners had taken again to drinking port with the lunch. On inquiry, young Esmond Baring said it had been his birthday, and he hoped this rule could be overlooked as a special favour. When Lancy did not seem to mind too much, partners' birthdays suddenly became a more frequent part of the social calendar.

With the onset of hostilities, most of the partners joined up, and with them most of the staff. The latter were helped on their way by a decision to dismiss all single men and recommend them for civil defence duties. Married men were told much the same, except that they were promised half their salaries as long as the firm continued to make profits (which, even in the leanest year of 1940, it continued to do). That left Lancy, the two Pitmans, Fitz Graham Watson, Andrew Vanneck and a core of around twenty staff, many of them women. However both Fred Pitman and Lancy were getting old. Pitman formally retired in March 1940, and almost exactly a year later Lancy died in harness. In his obituary, *The Times* noted that his 'intimate banking knowledge and sound judgement made him widely consulted. He possessed indeed a strong instinct for business and a facility for making quick decisions which seldom proved wrong.' Fred Pitman did not survive Lancy long, dying at his home in Hertfordshire in January 1942, aged 78. His memorial service at St Michael's, Cornhill, later that month was conducted by his cousin, the Reverend John Ellison, Rector of St Michael's and Chaplain in Ordinary to the King, whose son Gerald later became Bishop of London.

With Hugo Pitman as the new Senior Partner, the management was strengthened when Arthur Anderson returned, somewhat crestfallen, after two years in command of a training battalion, to tell his colleagues he had been 'bowler-hatted'. Of the clerks, Little and Palmer remained at Bishopsgate because, along with 'Gertie' Miller, Taffy Jones, Bill Owen and Arthur Hargrave, they were too old for military service. Constant Rayment and Kipper Herrington, who had both suffered from tuberculosis, were ruled out on medical grounds, as was Corney, who had a game leg – the consequences of childhood polio.

From the various battle-fronts came stories of considerable gallantry. Esmond Baring led the roll of honour. After joining the 4th County of London Yeomanry, he served with distinction in the Western Desert where he was Intelligence Officer with the 22nd Armoured Brigade during the Battle of Knightsbridge. Later, as Brigade-Major and General Staff Officer Intelligence with the Special Air Service, he was awarded the OBE, Legion of Honour and Croix de Guerre.

Elsewhere Ron Shubrook survived the sinking of the aircraft carrier HMS *Ark Royal* in November 1941. Reg Rogers had a similar experience but in more bizarre circumstances. In the autumn of 1942, he was serving on board the anti-aircraft cruiser HMS *Curacao* when she was involved in an appalling collision with the Cunard White Star liner *Queen Mary* which she was escorting across the Atlantic. The 80,000 ton *Queen Mary*, travelling at high speed, sliced through the 4,290-ton cruiser: out of nearly four hundred officers and men, only 26 were saved, among them Reg Rogers, who was picked up after four hours' immersion in an icy sea.

Back at Bishopsgate, there were heroics of a different kind. At the start of the Blitz, there was a general working rule that, as soon as an air-raid siren sounded, all books were taken down to the Hambros strong-room, where work would continue. This soon proved impracticable, so the work was carried on in the main office away from windows and the hazard of blasted glass. During one lengthy air raid Corney noticed three partners – Graham Watson, Vanneck and Anderson – huddled together in the cleaners' cupboard under the stairs. On further inspection, he found Hugo Pitman toiling away in the partners' working room,

The Camp Bird

where his deafness rendered him oblivious of any din and danger. Pitman refused all Corney's entreaties to take cover, only asking to be informed if the warning siren went off so that he could prepare himself to meet his maker. Luckily no direct hits occurred, and the Bishopsgate premises survived the war intact without any serious danger. (Sadly, this was not the case when an IRA bomb ravaged the City in 1994.)

For six years business was understandably depressed. Although savings were officially channelled into War Loan issues, several stockbrokers continued to float new companies, but Rowe & Pitman was not among them. Its most successful niche activity during the war was converting the Prudential's considerable assets into bonds.

Apart from the Blitz, 43 Bishopsgate had other links with the war effort. Hugo Pitman had his own distinguished military connections. Two cousins (the daughters of Fred Pitman) had married prominent soldiers – General Mason-Macfarlane, who led the British military mission to Moscow in 1941, and General Forbes-Adam, the Adjutant General to the forces. Mason-Macfarlane in particular was frequently on the phone to Rowe & Pitman. From time to time, Ian Fleming used to breeze in, wearing his naval commander's uniform, for lunch with Pitman. He would take the opportunity to ask Corney how the partners' profits were doing. (Unlike unmarried clerks, he continued – at Pitman's insistence – to draw his share.) Occasionally another young uniformed officer appeared. He was Hilary Bray, an Old Etonian nephew of Arthur Anderson, who was soon to join the firm. Corney remembers him introducing a distinguished guest, who turned out to be a nephew of China's Generalissimo Chiang Kai-shek, looking for legitimate British outlets for his wealth. As usual, Rowe & Pitman's connections were interesting and influential.

5 Stifling Red Tape

OF THE RED TAPE that threatened to stifle the City in the late 1940s, some was left over from the war, the rest introduced by the new Labour government. Erik Steffenberg, a partner in Hambros, spoke for many in the Square Mile when he observed in 1948, 'Business today does not only mean selling or buying – that may often be the easiest part – nor financing, but the most intricate and time-wasting labour is in complying with all the various regulations here and abroad.'

In this unpromising economic environment, Rowe & Pitman prospered more than most. There were three main reasons: first, a succession of typically Rowe & Pitman circumstances placed it in the financial vanguard when the Anglo American Corporation successfully expanded into South Africa's Orange Free State (OFS) from 1948; secondly, it was well placed to raise finance for some of the middle-level British companies that the Labour government wanted to support during its period in office from 1945 to 1951; and, thirdly, a bit later, it played a prominent role in the denationalization of the iron and steel industries in Britain after the Conservative Party was returned to power.

Two new partners were appointed in the year following the war. One was Hilary Bray, a charming, old-world figure who, for all his proficiency at golf and knowledge about birds and wild flowers, was not temperamentally suited to stockbroking. The other was Arthur Leveson, a Wykehamist who had been at Oxford with Harry Oppenheimer, the heir to the Anglo American Corporation and De Beers Consolidated Mines.

Leveson's appointment as partner in April 1946 followed shortly after the arrival of Comar Wilson to run Anglo American's London office in High Holborn. The tie between Rowe & Pitman and Anglo American was initiated by Lancy's brother, Lord Bicester, the senior Managing Director at Morgan Grenfell. Morgan's American parent, J.P. Morgan had been one of the original shareholders in Anglo (indeed, with Newmont Mining, the reason for the American half of the name). Morgan Grenfell had subsequently become Anglo's merchant bank. As Harry Oppenheimer bluntly put it, 'Bicester pushed us to Rowe & Pitman.'

Comar Wilson had already struck up a close friendship with Hughie Vivian Smith who – restless after an active war and sensing, perhaps, that, now his uncle was dead, the top job at Rowe & Pitman would never be his – decided abruptly to leave stockbroking and join Anglo American. For Rowe & Pitman this created an opportunity. Leveson's arrival at Bishopsgate created a personal link to the very top of Anglo which was looking for finance for the development of deep-level gold mining in the OFS. Working closely with Vivian Smith, Esmond Baring spearheaded an operation which, between 1948 and 1952 raised all the £39 million required for various stages of the OFS Goldfields development. The money came entirely from UK institutions, without the intermediation of any merchant bank – a hugely impressive feat in anyone's book. There were mixed feelings at Rowe & Pitman when, towards the end of 1951, Baring decided for personal reasons to join his friend Vivian Smith at Anglo. Fortunately, his move had entirely positive repercussions for the firm. With Vivian Smith at the helm of various Oppenheimer businesses in South Africa and Baring as Anglo's Executive Director in London, Rowe & Pitman's role in the development of South African mining was only enhanced.

It was a time of institutional change within Rowe & Pitman. Following the bureaucratic turmoil which followed the death of Harry Little in 1947, the partnership decided the following year, after over half a century in existence, to dissolve itself and reform as a limited company. There were two main reasons for this:

on the one hand, profits had to be distributed under partnership law, so there was no way, especially in the prevailing political climate, of building up assets; on the other, the cost of joining the partnership was becoming too expensive for young men without substantial resources, particularly as they had to pay tax in advance on their initial earnings.

These changes encouraged a further shake-up in senior management. (We shall continue to call them 'partners' because the new scheme failed to take off and Rowe & Pitman reverted to a partnership in December 1956.) Like Vivian Smith, Fleming had never been cut out for stockbroking and, after an eventful war, decided to call it a day. Chitty and Vanneck also retired over the next few years, leaving vacancies for three new partners in the late 1940s – Wilfred de Knoop, Jim Graham Watson and Julian Martin Smith. Another Morgan Grenfell protégé, de Knoop maintained the firm's formal contacts with important Scottish institutional clients, although, on a day-to-day basis, his colleagues valued him rather more for his intimate knowledge of the *Guide Michelin*. Known as the gastronomic partner, he would despatch a messenger to Twinings in the Strand every Friday to buy freshly roasted coffee for his weekend in the country.

In the Rowe & Pitman tradition of promoting family ties wherever possible, Jim Graham Watson was the nephew of 'Fitz', the man with an ex-officio seat in the Hambros boardroom. (Fitz liked to start his sentences with the words, 'My spies tell me. . . .' When that happened everyone knew he was about to impart a piece of intelligence gleaned from Hambros.) A product of Eton and Cambridge, the young Graham Watson spent some time learning the ropes with Hilary Bray in the firm's gilts department before getting the other partners' support for his plans to develop the firm's limited research capacity.

Another nephew (and namesake of the partner killed at the start of the First World War), Martin Smith was a Hambro through and through. Having worked at Myers, a smaller broker used by both Hambros and Rowe & Pitman, he was recommended by his uncle Olaf Hambro, chairman of Hambros Bank, who may have been concerned at the growing Morgan Grenfell influence at the 'family broker'. But since this 'Mark II' Martin Smith was to become an influential Senior Partner, his story belongs to a later era.

The new recruits found that the prevailing economic circumstances favoured different ways of raising capital from before the war. The partners still did the daily round of the merchant banks which, if anything, were more eager than ever to promote new issues. As for distribution, the pre-war vogue for investment trusts and syndicates was waning. Pension funds and insurance companies were now more important than ever as outlets for stockbrokers like Rowe & Pitman. Very few issues of any size were attempted without calling on the Holborn 'club' comprising the major insurance companies, particularly the Prudential, Pearl, Legal and General, Royal Exchange and Commercial Union. However, getting the 'club' on board was still a very amateur business. More often than not, it meant going down the list of underwriters and telling the investment manager at a particular insurance company, 'We've put you down for 50 [thousand shares].'

At the same time, private clients were no longer as important to stockbrokers as before. In 1948/9, they accounted for only 10 per cent of Rowe & Pitman's commissions of £202,060. Young bloods like Jim Graham Watson could see that servicing an average client dealing in £500 trades was expensive and time-consuming. Gilt-edged business, on the other hand, required few overheads and was profitable. Over the next five years total gilt-edged commissions rose from £46,021 to £105,020.

As in earlier times, Rowe & Pitman still needed banks and issuing houses to generate business. As Lancy's heir (he inherited The Old Hall at Garboldisham), and for as long as he remained with the firm, Esmond Baring could count on Helbert Wagg to push a sizeable proportion of its post-war new company issues through Rowe & Pitman. Like Fitz Graham Watson, Baring also enjoyed a productive relationship with Hambros.

Fitz was in a class of his own, however, when it came to working with the new Industrial and Commercial Finance Company which the Labour government had set up to provide small businesses with up to £200,000 in medium- and long-term capital. Fitz developed a close personal friendship with J.B. Kinross, a fellow Edinburgh man, who ran the ICFC and (from 1953) its related Estate Duties Investment trust (EDITH). In his memoirs, *Fifty Years in the City,* Kinross recalled working with Fitz when Mutual Finance, a small quoted hire-purchase company in which ICFC had a stake, was being courted by four different parties. Eventually another Rowe & Pitman client, Thomas Tilling, agreed to pay 20s for the company, or roughly double its recent price. Through ICFC's chairman, Lord Piercy, Rowe & Pitman was introduced to the Kuwait Investment Office, which handled the emirate's world-wide investments – a massive account when oil prices took off in the 1970s. Meanwhile Arthur Anderson proved his worth by attracting a significant amount of the iron and steel privatization business to Rowe & Pitman.

It has to be admitted that the partners' political persuasions were never much in doubt. One of Jim Graham Watson's earliest 'corporate' memories is accompanying Esmond Baring, Arthur Leveson and Wilfred de Knoop to canvas for the Conservatives in the February 1950 election in the East Islington constituency abutting the City.

Following Hugo Pitman's resignation in March 1951, Anderson became Chairman of the company, to use the precise terminology of those few years. (Fitz Graham Watson, the other candidate for the job, was considered too pedantic by the new younger partners. Pitman continued as a director, then partner, until the early 1960s.) A couple of years later, Anderson's friendship with Sir John Morison of Thomson McLintock, the accountancy firm with long links with Rowe & Pitman, paid dividends when the latter was appointed Chairman of the Iron and Steel Holding and Realisation Agency to supervise the denationalization programme. The issuing houses, which were underwriting the various flotations, then appointed six brokers to sell the various shares, starting with United Steel in November 1953. Since Rowe & Pitman had worked on pre-war issues for United Steel and was close to Morgan Grenfell, bankers to five of the big six steel companies, the other brokers were happy to let Rowe & Pitman do most of the work and fill most of the allotments. Fees were good, and continued so for some time. But whether the operation can be considered a long-term success is debatable. Although the privatized steel shares, with their higher than average yield, were generally welcomed by market observers, they were overshadowed by the Labour Party's threat to renationalize them when it returned to power. For a year, at least, steel shares tended to trade at a discount. Although they improved as investments, they were indeed taken back into public ownership in the British Steel Corporation following Labour's general election victory in 1966.

Inside Rowe & Pitman, the complicated nature of the steel issues called for bureaucratic sophistication, particularly in preparing prospectuses and keeping books. Where Little had once reigned supreme, Bill Palmer, the Office Manager, now supervised the drafting and circulation of fast-changing underwriting lists, while Simon Rodney acted as a temporary security chief, responsible for preventing rival brokers from stealing new clients from these valuable documents.

One purchaser of United Steel stock was Rowe & Pitman's old client Lord Beaverbrook. During the couple of decades following Lancy's heyday in the 1920s, the newspaper magnate lost interest in the stock market. Then, in April 1954, he wrote to Hugo Pitman saying that, for reasons of old age, he wanted to sell a block of 2 million non-voting A Ordinary Shares in London Express Newspapers (shortly to be called Beaverbrook Newspapers). He wanted Rowe & Pitman's help in selling the shares (worth around £2 million), partly so that he could endow a charitable foundation providing scholarships for Canadians in Britain.

Pitman being away in Ireland, Fitz Graham Watson replied with three suggestions as to how Beaverbrook could achieve his aim. He could sell the shares to the general public on a prospectus, he could offer them to other shareholders at a discount, or they 'could be bought at a net price by a small group who would subsequently arrange for the placing or marketing of such number as they might not wish to retain for permanent investment'. Fitz recommended the latter course as being 'quicker and almost certainly less expensive'.

When Fitz and Hilary Bray went to see Beaverbrook, they learned that he had decided to sell only 1 million of these shares. A contemporary note by Beaverbrook's assistant, A.G. Millar, is revealing about Rowe & Pitman's *modus operandi* at the time:

> Mr Graham Watson said that he had in mind a small syndicate among Institutions and Finance Houses, with whom they had close relations. He felt that they would undoubtedly retain shares for investment purposes, but others they might market in their own time, and from their own point of view they would only do it when it would not affect the market to their own detriment.

In the event Rowe & Pitman put together a small syndicate of leading financial houses, supported by a secondary distribution through a much wider clientele. Referring to roughly a quarter of the transfers lodged by Rowe & Pitman, Millar noted that the shares went to:

34 individuals (of whom F. Grant QC 3000 shares)	28,500
1 college at Cambridge	2,000
9 Investment Trusts or Insurance companies	89,000
sundry bank nominees	110,500
total	230,000

Beaverbrook's renewed interest in the stock market reflected the boom which, at Rowe & Pitman, saw commissions jump from little more than £200,000 to over £700,000 during the 1950s. Only Rodney and Fitz Graham Watson retired during this period, but such was the volume of business that seven people were hired to replace them. W.T. (Peter) Henderson arrived at the start of the decade, recommended by Hugo Pitman and Arthur Anderson. A modern languages scholar from Cambridge, he was the logical choice to lead Rowe & Pitman's expansion into

Europe, which came as part of a general drive overseas in the early 1960s. In the meantime, Henderson was usefully employed as the link man with provincial stockbrokers, still an important source of business for the firm.

In 1951, following Esmond Baring's departure to Anglo American, Tom Leveson Gower, a jobber with Sambourne, was recruited to strengthen the ranks of middle management. Already forty-eight years old and a kinsman of the Duke of Sutherland, he had formerly worked for Morgan Grenfell where he retained many useful contacts. With his natural diplomacy, he soon became something of an elder statesman, taking on the role of Senior Partner for a short period between Arthur Anderson's retirement in 1966 and the emergence of his real successor Julian Martin Smith a couple of years later.

A younger candidate who would play an important role in the next stage of Rowe & Pitman's expansion was quickly identified in Bill Mackworth-Young, an energetic and imaginative former Oppidan scholar at Eton, who joined the firm in October 1953. Aged twenty-seven, he had spent three years in the Welsh Guards, before serving a short City apprenticeship at Barings.

Ro Wadham, an Oxford graduate, had won a wartime DFC in the Fleet Air Arm. Still only thirty-one when he came to Rowe & Pitman in 1954, his experience at Nathan & Rosselli, one of the City's smaller brokers, made him particularly adept at nurturing the less substantial, but still profitable, corporate relationships which increasingly provided bread-and-butter business for firms like Rowe & Pitman. When Fitz retired in 1957, Wadham took on responsibility for working with the ICFC. Guided by Bill Corney, who more than ever was the local arbiter of Stock Exchange rules, he was involved in notable issues, such as Lee Cooper.

The remaining three partners who joined in the 1950s were Michael Bonsor, an able recruit from the dark horse, S.G. Warburg; William Robson, a former Royal Navy man who helped push Rowe & Pitman into the Far East; and David Innes, who arrived in 1955 with an agriculture degree from Cambridge. The ward of Tom Leveson Gower, Innes took control of the firm's gilt-edged business, and later – as Finance Partner – played a crucial role in the firm's development, as he made sure that Rowe & Pitman operated as smoothly and professionally as any other multi-million pound City business.

Like most of the younger intake, Innes had to spend three years learning the ropes before becoming a partner. Such trainees were known as 'Orchids' because they were 'generally a delicately scented, highly decorative, well-bred specially cultivated species; sometimes of grotesque shape and of little practical use'. Others who passed through this exclusive induction course (originally instigated by Lancy) included Lord Charles Cavendish, who married Fred Astaire's sister Adèle, Lord Herbert, Arnold John Hugh Smith, the golfer Roger Wethered, the cricketer Errol Holmes, who joined Chase Securities Corporation, Derek Wood, a nephew of Alfred Wagg, Eddie Grant, a Captain of School at Eton, Alex Abel Smith, later a director of Schroder Wagg and Chairman of Pressed Steel, Charlie Gundy, who became Senior Partner of Wood Gundy in Toronto, Charles Hambro, later Lord Hambro and seventh Chairman of Hambros Bank, and Julian Ogilvie Thompson, a Rhodes scholar who went on to Anglo American and chairmanship of De Beers.

In the 1980s, one such recruit, working as a novice in the transfer department, was shown the door after creating a stamp with the words 'May the fleas of a thousand camels infest your arsehole' and using it to validate a £100 million gilts order from the Kuwait Investment Office. Around this time Viscount Althorp (later Earl Spencer, the brother of the late Diana, Princess of Wales) also spent some time in the office, but only as a holiday job.

By the end of the 1950s, the outlines of modern Stock Exchange procedures could be discerned. Starting with the 1948 Companies Act, which introduced modern habits of disclosure, the privileged old boys' club of pre-war years was showing signs of the more open, dynamic market which served until the 'Big Bang' of 1986.

As company broker, and as intermediary between banks and issuing houses on the one hand, and insurance companies, pensions funds and other institutions on the other, Rowe & Pitman was involved in several notable issues during this decade, from Imperial Tobacco's £20 million loan stock in October 1950 to Shell's £40 million rights in February 1958. By most measures – from numbers of issues to general sentiment – Rowe & Pitman was at that time one of the top three stockbrokers in London (a position it shared with Cazenove and Hoare and Company).

Hubris of a kind came with the celebrated 'aluminium wars' of 1958-9, when Rowe & Pitman found itself in the embarrassing position of acting on both sides of the bid for British Aluminium by Reynolds Metals of Virginia, reputedly the first hostile takeover in the City of London. In the process, the firm demonstrated that it was not as nimble-footed as it liked to think. In modern parlance, it had much to learn about being street-wise.

Rowe & Pitman's links with British Aluminium were long established and well oiled. Cunliffe interests still dominated at the industrial giant, where Robert Cooper was Chairman after retiring as a Rowe & Pitman partner in 1928. Although the Cunliffes had shifted their allegiance to Cazenove when Claud Serocold moved there, Rowe & Pitman (in the shape of Fitz Graham Watson) still looked after certain Cunliffe family investments. Indeed Fitz's first cousin, Geoffrey Cunliffe, a son of the ex-Governor of the Bank of England, was Managing Director of British Aluminium. To square the circle, Hambros was the company's merchant bank.

However, through Helbert Wagg, Rowe & Pitman was also broker to Tube Investments, Reynolds Metals' British partner in the takeover bid. Initially, Rowe & Pitman thought it could act for both sides. But when Hambros, acting with Lazards, made it quite clear that 'he that was not for them was against them', the firm had to make up its mind. Understandably, for historical and sentimental reasons, it opted to back British Aluminium, which was supported by a formidable array of the City's top financial institutions. As token of his intent, Arthur Anderson placed his nephew Hilary Bray in charge of the defence.

In the event the Reynolds-Tube Investments consortium won, partly because it had the larger purse, and partly because it was advised by the inventive S.G. Warburg, still something of an unknown quantity as a merchant bank. The whole saga has been represented in retrospect as a watershed: a victory for the nimble-footed outsiders over the otiose City establishment. For Rowe & Pitman it was a painful learning experience, though Tube Investments soon returned as a client, and soon it was possible to view events more positively. As the firm's friend Lionel Fraser, Chairman of Helbert Wagg, recorded in his 1963 autobiography, *All to the Good*:

> I believe the British Aluminium affair provoked a remarkable transformation in the City. Old citadels tumbled, traditional strongholds were invaded, new thought was devoted to City problems, there was a freshness and alertness unknown before, dramatic to watch. And this transformation has been achieved whilst old relationships have been resumed, differences have been forgotten and new alliances have been made. Everything has long since been tranquil and harmonious, nevertheless it is different.

6 Moving On

IN 1958 ROWE & PITMAN finally summoned the courage to leave its 'temporary' accommodation above Hambros Bank at 43 Bishopsgate. It had been there nearly forty years, and for much of that time Hugo Pitman had talked of finding new offices. But, to the consternation of the junior Hambros partners who coveted Rowe & Pitman's two floors, he always managed to postpone the dreadful day. The reason soon became clear: at Bishopsgate, Rowe & Pitman paid a peppercorn rent; for Bucklersbury House, its new premises at 3 Queen Victoria Street in the shadow of Mansion House, it was charged what at the time seemed an outrageous £5 5s 6d per square foot. According to an almost contemporary account by Ian Nairn, the architectural historian, 'This mass of building has a lot of storeys, a lot of windows, freedom from pointlessly applied period detail, freedom from obvious gracelessness, freedom from aesthetic megalomania. It has no virtues and no vices: it is the null point of architecture.'

But the premises were new (built in 1954), were independent, and were to act as a base from which Rowe & Pitman could build during the turbulent 1960s. It was a curious period because – *pace* Lionel Fraser – the firm still had not given much thought to its role in a big bad world of hostile takeovers. In 1962 Hilary Bray thought he could ask his 'Uncle Arthur' if he could come to a new arrangement with the firm because he wanted to do 'very much less work'. Since he was not the most industrious of partners, his offer was rejected, and he retired from the firm to pursue more agreeable country pursuits. His close friend Bill Mackworth-Young later wrote of him:

> To tell the truth, he wasn't a very good stockbroker. Apart from the delight he took in seeing daily some of his many friends both inside and outside the firm, and a genuine concern for the welfare of his clients, his heart wasn't in it. Business competition – perhaps any kind of competition – went against his nature, he would speak disparagingly of 'grubbing in the money-pile', and it may be that he regretted more deeply than his partners the quickening pace of life in the City of London, where the newer god Success was coming to be worshipped equally with the older god Probity.

At the start of the decade, the veteran Hugo Pitman still used to come into the office regularly. One of his responsibilities was as trustee (with Seymour Egerton of Coutts) to the Queen Mother's marriage settlement, which at the time was modestly valued at just under £30,000. Informed by Ferguson, the clerk in charge of the Private Clients Department, that the terms of the trust were not written in stone and that he might improve the capital by switching half out of fixed-interest securities into equities, Pitman did not exactly turn his deaf ear but answered in a clipped tone, 'There's no point in making any recommendations. She'll only spend it.'

This attitude was reflected in the senior management of Arthur Anderson and Tom Leveson Gower, who were essentially reactionary and unwilling to contemplate radical innovation. In two particular areas, however, Rowe & Pitman was indeed changing, and the impetus was coming from its lower ranks: it was developing its own independent research, and it was hungry for new business overseas.

The in-house research department grew from Jim Graham Watson's promptings. Despite Nicholas Davenport's early efforts, Rowe & Pitman's capacity in this field was limited. Most investment suggestions were made on the basis of a company's dividend record, supplemented by occasional advice received from the market. If, on examining a client's list of securities, a partner was ignorant about a particular company, he would ask the House clerks to obtain details from a firm of jobbers, who tended to keep records of companies whose stocks they dealt in. This was a haphazard way of gathering intelligence because a jobber's views could be coloured by the state of his book.

Graham Watson set about changing this. An early practitioner of the dark arts of investment analysis, he had plotted company performances on graph paper in the late 1940s. When the Statistical Department was initiated in 1954, it only consisted of Graham Watson and his deputy, Eric Fry. They recruited two graduates, John Lewington and Derek Harding, who helped build up the firm's expertise in specific market sectors, such as electricals and stores. This information was then circulated to fund managers to help them choose their investments.

Before long Rowe & Pitman was managing the Rolls Royce, Ford and Diamond Trading Company pension funds, and advising many others, including the Stock Exchange's own one, which appears suggestively in Graham Watson's diaries as 'Sexpen'. The firm's investment suggestions were appreciated by longer-standing clients, like the insurance companies and the old Thomson McClintock vehicle, the Grange Trust, where Graham Watson was appointed a director in November 1960. Eric Fry's meticulously researched book, *Comparative Dividend and Earnings Records*, which ran to ten editions, won widespread plaudits the same year. When Rowe & Pitman was asked to advise several new municipal pension funds such as Portsmouth's and West Ham's, Graham Watson felt he was really getting somewhere.

Even so, inside Bucklersbury House, there remained large pockets of resistance to talk of price-earnings ratios and equivalent realized redemption yields. Arthur Anderson refused to allow 'Stats' to call itself the Research Department. This institutional myopia meant that the statistical team was forced to keep to itself within the firm.

As a former naval man, Graham Watson's solution was to press for a central operations room, where his team's intelligence could be incorporated with other information, such as new issue prospectuses and the latest Stock Exchange prices, and disseminated to a wider audience. During 1960 he was emboldened to write a memorandum entitled 'Proposed New Section' which, while studiously avoiding references to anything so radical as an 'ops room', nevertheless called for a 'central clearing section' to provide a better service to institutional clients. Despite the considerable capital outlay involved, by the end of the year the office partitions on the seventh floor were being moved to make way for an Operations Room.

The previous year, James D'Albiac, a young graduate who was to make a significant mark on the Statistical (and later Research) Department, had joined the firm as an 'orchid'. His connection was that his father was Air Marshal John D'Albiac, whose Aide-de-Camp had been Aubrey Baring, brother of Esmond. After Winchester, the young D'Albiac read PPE at Magdalen College, Oxford. Numerate and intellectually precocious, but uncertain as to his future career, he was taken by his father to lunch at the Anglo American Corporation where Julian Martin Smith, Esmond Baring and Arthur Leveson were also present. Martin Smith told him there might be an opening at Rowe & Pitman, but he was not to get a first (a good stockbroker should not be that brainy) and he was always to remember to wear a bowler hat.

D'Albiac did the usual training course – one year in the back office, filling in forms, dealing with telephone customers and learning the rudiments of stockbroking under the watchful eye of the then Office Manager, Constant Rayment and his assistant A.C. Hargrave; one year as a dealer 'in the box' in the Stock Exchange; and one year in the Statistical Department, under Jim Graham Watson. However, D'Albiac did not play the game according to the rules. At Oxford, he had been known as 'Nimble Ninepence' in recognition of his profitable stock market speculations on behalf of his friends. His period 'in the box' honed these skills, with the result that, during his third year, he spent rather too much time on the telephone discussing tips with his friends. No one was too surprised when, after three years, he was sacked and marked down as 'NPM' – not partner material.

Rowe & Pitman was a notably *laisser-faire* outfit during this period. (Several partners recall how, as new recruits, they were left to their own devices to find a niche that was useful to the firm.) So D'Albiac refused to leave. He hung around Bucklersbury House until he was taken on again as a humble clerk in the Statistical Department. Realizing that he had to make himself indispensable, he decided to revive the *Securities for Investment* circulars (now called *Market Reports*) which Ian Fleming had last written in the 1930s. His first effort in 1962 was produced by Roneo, but the following year his *Market Report* became a properly printed document with a witty, informed editorial, charts, comments about market conditions at home and abroad, and even share recommendations. The publication, which ran till February 1985, proved an invaluable tool, not only in encouraging the various disciplines in the Operations Room to coalesce, but also in reaching out to the new breed of investment managers which was beginning to take important decisions throughout the City.

Old ways persisted in the City in the early 1960s, it is true. The directors of the merchant banks, in particular, valued their personal relationships with Rowe & Pitman partners. When James Ogilvy joined as an 'orchid' in 1959, the same year as D'Albiac, the partners still religiously conducted their daily rounds of the merchant bank boardrooms. First they would pick up the prices from the Rowe & Pitman office. Then they would go their separate ways – Leveson Gower and Mackworth-Young to Morgan Grenfell (which provided nearly half the business at the time), Martin Smith to Hambros (the family connection), de Knoop to Lazards and Wadham to the Charterhouse Group. (The existing Morgan Grenfell link had been boosted by Esmond Baring, who was brother-in-law of Lord Harcourt, Managing Director of the merchant bank from 1931 to 1968 and later Lord Bicester's successor as Chairman. Rowe & Pitman's Lazards connection, which had earlier been neglected, also benefited from its network of family and corporate ties. For Julian Ogilvie Thompson, who had passed through Rowe & Pitman as an 'orchid' in the mid-1950s, and who went on to chair the Anglo American group, was married to a daughter of Lord Hampden, the bank's chairman.) Most partners enjoyed this diurnal ritual of visiting the merchant banks, and thus one reason for internal opposition to the Operations Room, which was clearly designed to do them out of this job and, if its logic was followed through, to by-pass or at least duplicate the role of the merchant banks.

The third son of the ninth Earl of Airlie, Ogilvy came to Rowe & Pitman with impeccable City connections. One brother David was to become Chairman of Schroders in 1977, while the other worked for Harley Drayton's conglomerate at 117 Old Broad Street and was shortly to join the board of Lonrho. A former Page of Honour to King George VI, Ogilvy had been employed by both Read Hurst-Brown and Panmure Gordon, before being introduced to Rowe & Pitman through his brother-in-law Lord Lloyd's best friend, Esmond Baring.

Since he already knew several members of the board at Morgan Grenfell, Ogilvy looked forward to being presented there. But Tom Leveson Gower refused to take him to meet the bank directors until Ogilvy discarded his 'pyjamas' (in reality, his striped shirt) and wore the regulation stiff collar. After being forced to conform, Ogilvy recounted his story of what he considered unnecessarily stuffy behaviour to Tim Collins, one of Morgan Grenfell's younger directors, who agreed to participate in a joke. The next day, when Leveson Gower paid his customary call to the bank, Collins asked him – apropos of Ogilvy – why Rowe & Pitman suffered a partner who neglected to clean his shoes. Leveson Gower did not need any further prompting: as soon as he returned to his own office, he summoned Ogilvy and ordered him never to appear in public with dirty shoes again. (On a different sartorial note, the exotic post-1960s development of female fashions was viewed askance by some partners, and on one occasion a secretary was sent home because her skirt was allegedly too short.)

Ogilvy arrived at Rowe & Pitman at more or less exactly the same time as Peter Wilmot-Sitwell and David Brooke, two more Old Etonians who were to play vital roles in chivvying the firm to move with the times over the next couple of decades. Wilmot-Sitwell had known Ogilvy from childhood, and once amused the latter's mother by writing to her as Mrs Airlie. After Oxford and a short period at Hambros Bank, he joined Rowe & Pitman in 1959 on the recommendation of Comar Wilson from Anglo American's London office. (Wilson was a friend of Wilmot-Sitwell's mother, who hailed from one of New Zealand's richest industrial families, the Fishers. At Oxford he had gone out with Wilson's daughter Caroline.)

Quickly slated as a coming young man, Wilmot-Sitwell was only twenty-five when he was made a partner in April 1960. With Bill Mackworth-Young, who was already a partner, he and Ogilvy began pressing for Graham Watson's Operations Room, but from a different perspective. As Ogilvy in particular saw it, the servicing of private clients had all but dried up, but corporate business was 'beginning to get quite interesting'. To make the most of this growing market, Rowe & Pitman needed to capitalize on its proven placing power with the institutions. But the firm was held back by bureaucratic inertia.

The young bloods saw the Operations Room as a way of improving at least part of this administrative impasse, so that research could feed into new issues, as well as to sales advice to institutions. Consequently the Operations Room became rather more than even Graham Watson had envisaged. With its communal white plasticated board, its red, blue and black pens to denote buy, sell and hold recommendations of shares and, later, its Reuter screens, it was to become the sales room, not to say the nerve centre, of the firm's entire corporate activity.

Meanwhile another process – the globalization of the firm's business – was starting to happen elsewhere. Until the Second World War, overseas had meant only the United States. Rowe & Pitman had been involved in international issues, it is true, such as mining shares in South Africa or Australia and sovereign debt in South America or even Eastern Europe. But these had all been initiated and serviced out of London, the world's financial capital. Rowe & Pitman made no effort to find clients or business in these parts of the world.

The United States was a little different. The firm's link with J.P. Morgan had given it an important entrée to American clients, particularly after the First World War. Sidney Russell Cooke visited the United States and Canada in May and June 1929. His diary recorded details of an exhausting social life as he rode, sailed, played tennis, and acquainted himself with the new talking pictures. He also managed to make contact with many of the leading financial firms including Dillon Read, Brown Brothers and Wood Gundy, as well as visit the Ford factory in Detroit where he witnessed 106,000 employees producing ninety-five cars an hour on a 'drive off' assembly line some 850 ft in length.

After Cooke's death in 1930, Hugo Pitman became responsible for American business, and clearly enjoyed his regular autumn jaunts across the Atlantic on one of the Cunard liners. But no concerted effort was made to pitch for American clients, and the introduction of the dollar premium after the war dampened any enthusiasm to rush into US equities. When David Brooke joined Rowe & Pitman in 1959, the City of London and Wall Street seemed as far apart as they had ever been. Anyone wanting to telephone the United States had to obtain permission from senior management and book the call an hour in advance. Coded quotations crossed the Atlantic by cable, with four different companies competing for the favour of carrying the traffic.

By that time the aggressive encroachment of some American broking firms into Britain during the 1950s had caused some reassessment. After his basic training, Brooke, a suave, personable linguist who had lived in the United States after the war, was seconded to New York for a year to train with G.H. Walker, a leading Wall Street stockbroker, whose senior partner at the time was 'Herbie' Walker, an uncle of George Bush, who later became President of the United States. Returning to Rowe & Pitman in London, Brooke began researching American companies for Michael Bonsor, the partner officially responsible for overseas operations.

During the 1960s, it became clear that substantial company growth was taking place not in Britain, but abroad, particularly in the United States. But Rowe & Pitman clients were held back from investing in the United States because they had to pay double commission – to the London firm as per usual and to the American broker which executed its orders. Two events in 1967 encouraged Rowe & Pitman to think of establishing its own presence in the United States. One was the devaluation of the pound, which reduced the importance of the sterling area to British investors. The other was the news that its main rival Cazenove was buying a seat on the Pacific Coast Stock Exchange in San Francisco.

Rowe & Pitman decided to follow suit. The New York Stock Exchange was still closed to foreign firms, but San Francisco was more welcoming. There the firm could execute its own orders (thus reducing its fees to its clients). In addition, it could build up its own in-house expertise in American securities, while by-passing the dollar premium market would make it more competitive in the management of off-shore funds.

Funded by $165,000 of 'dollar premium' currency and borrowing a further $50,000 from Barclays Bank in San Francisco, Rowe & Pitman opened a San Francisco office with a seat at the Pacific Stock Exchange in May 1968. At the height of the Vietnam War, a high-level team comprising Bonsor, Brooke, Corney, Mackworth-Young and Martin Smith (who had recently become Senior Partner) travelled to the West Coast where a lavish party signalled the arrival of Rowe & Pitman Inc. A memo from Corney survives, recording his impressions of the sights and sounds of San Francisco, and adding, 'I kept repeating that our main object was to give our clients a better service at a cheaper price, but I didn't quite appreciate what this meant until it was pointed out to me that on one of our first deals our client was charged £18 for commission whereas the previous week he would have been charged £78.'

The firm's cramped new premises at 111 Pine Street were originally run by Reginald Monkhouse, a former Shell executive with excellent local contacts, while Ann di Giorgio, the indefatigable Office Manager, provided logistical support. Monkhouse was joined by Nelson Weller, an experienced analyst, who soon impressed with his astute reports on California companies, particularly in the emerging Silicon Valley. One of the office's first tasks was to produce a study of two supermarket groups: the established Lucky Stores, with a strong market valuation and many followers, and the then lacklustre Safeway Stores, which had just taken on new management. Surprisingly, Lucky emerged as a 'sell' and Safeway a 'buy'. The Scottish institutions accepted this advice and did well from it.

That year Brooke became a partner and began to take a more general overview of Rowe & Pitman's international operations. The following year he invited David Russell to help him run Rowe & Pitman's United States subsidiary. Initially Russell (himself the scion of an established City dynasty, since both his father and grandfather had headed the family firm later known as Henderson Crosthwaite) was loath to leave his then American firm because he was sceptical about Rowe & Pitman's prospects. Brooke prevailed on him, and Russell joined, initially in San Francisco.

Rowe & Pitman Inc. took off in the late 1970s, helped on its way by the ending of British exchange controls in 1979 and by the business of two substantial clients, Fidelity Management Research of Boston and the Kuwait Investment Office (KIO). Fidelity, the largest mutual fund group in the United States, was Russell's first significant account. For its initial venture overseas, the Fidelity Pacific Fund, Rowe & Pitman raised $25 million from UK institutions, a considerable sum at the time. Meanwhile, the KIO was enjoying the substantial fruits of the mid-1970s rise in the price of oil. Rowe & Pitman Inc. was responsible for several of the Office's successful venture capital investments in the United States, among them United Asset Management, until a stake in Ogle, an oil-production company, went wrong, and the relationship soured. Nevertheless the substantial cash flow generated by KIO business was an important factor in helping Rowe & Pitman to expand in the face of fierce local competition.

In the rest of the world, Australia had long been the preserve of Simon Rodney. When Lazards and Morgan Grenfell had formed a new merchant bank, Australian United Corporation, in the early 1950s, Rodney encouraged Rowe & Pitman to take a closer interest, becoming broker to their new joint investment trust, the London Australia Investment Company. Bill Mackworth-Young had come to the partnership from Australia United at Rodney's behest and, following the latter's retirement in 1957, took charge of all business in the antipodes, travelling there regularly, raising money for companies such as BHP and prestigious developments including Australia Square in Sydney.

Mackworth-Young already had a link to the firm through his wife Eve's father, the Earl of Rothes, who was a close friend of Hugo Pitman. But he quickly made his own mark. A former Oppidan scholar at Eton, he had a fine classical brain, which could quickly analyse a problem and decide on appropriate action – whether it was the construction of a model electric railway, incorporating an infallible points and signals system, for Peter Henderson's children, or an evaluation of the Japanese loans system, with its complex gold and dollar clauses and accumulated arrears distilled into a brilliant analysis.

On his trips to Australia, Mackworth-Young was often accompanied by William Robson, who had spent twelve years in the Royal Navy before joining Rowe & Pitman in 1957, becoming a partner two years later. Robson began pressing the firm to take more interest in business opportunities in the Far East, where he had personal connections: he had spent two years of his naval service in Hong Kong where, for three generations, his wife's family had been associated with the leading trading house, Jardine Matheson.

At the end of their 1962 Australasian tour Mackworth-Young and Robson were deputed to visit both Hong Kong and Japan, which was where the partners were convinced the real Far Eastern opportunities lay. When Japan proved a closed shop, Rowe & Pitman began using Jardine Matheson's International Pacific Securities Company as a vehicle to invest there. Before long the firm had developed close links with the Hong Kong brokers, Mok Ying Kie, and was investing directly in Jardine Matheson on behalf of institutional clients. In 1971 it acted as joint sub-underwriter to Jardine's mammoth Hong Kong Land issue.

For a while the partnership proved resistant to the idea of setting up its own office in the Far East. But after London stockbrokers such as W.I. Carr and Vickers da Costa established a presence, the tide slowly turned. After visiting Hong Kong in December 1971, James Ogilvy and David Brooke advised that Rowe & Pitman should establish a representative office there – an opinion which was reinforced by William Robson and Nigel Elwes a couple of months later.

Elwes, a nephew of Julian Martin Smith, was Rowe & Pitman's first trained accountant: after leaving Cambridge he had taken articles with Sydenham and Company in 1961. He joined the firm seven years later, becoming a partner in April 1971. Internationalist in outlook, he was bullish about the Far East. But at that stage he was not willing to jeopardize his newly acquired status by working abroad. So it was not until 1975 that Richard Bonsor, a young cousin of Julian Martin Smith (and nephew of Michael Bonsor), agreed to set up an office in Hong Kong – officially, Rowe & Pitman (Far East) Ltd, with a capital of £10,000. An Old Etonian, Bonsor had joined Rowe & Pitman straight from Oxford in October 1968, and had worked as an 'orchid', initially in the Research Department under D'Albiac. In the colony he was supported by two able women: one was his attractive wife Susie (together they formed a glamorous couple famously described in Hong Kong as 'the Innocents Abroad'), and the other Pandora Wong, a most capable secretary who had been with Vickers da Costa.

Having negotiated membership of the Kam Ngam Stock Exchange on favourable terms, the Hong Kong office quickly earned its keep. Low tax rates allowed money to be kept in the colony on deposit. With retentions there and in the United States, Rowe & Pitman found, to the relief of the dwindling core of internal doubters, that it could fund its foreign operations without recourse to general partnership capital. At this stage Rowe & Pitman could be said to be a truly international business – epitomized by the fact that Bonsor's first big trade was purchasing South African mining shares for local Hong Kong institutions through Rowe & Pitman's Johannesburg office.

Moving On

Ironically, while wavering about Hong Kong, Rowe & Pitman almost established a presence in Tehran. In 1973 David Brooke had visited the Iranian capital as part of an official UK invisible exports team. At the time the Shah was thinking about opening a stock exchange. As a result Brooke and Richard Southby, another accountant (ex-Coopers & Lybrand) who had become a partner the previous year, were invited back to write a report on the future for capital markets in Iran. Although Brooke did his best to lose his report (the fruit of three months' work) in Boodles, Rowe & Pitman was invited to open an office in Tehran, with its expenses underwritten by the Shah's Pahlavi Foundation. Nothing came of this initiative, though trainees from Iran's National Investment Corporation passed through Rowe & Pitman's offices for a few years afterwards.

Apart from Europe, the firm's other great overseas interest – a long-standing one – was South Africa. The key here was the Oppenheimer connection which, ably handled by first-rate lieutenants, had created an unusual harmony of interests between Rowe & Pitman and the Anglo American/De Beers empire. These links were strengthened in 1969 when, during a visit to Johannesburg, Julian Martin Smith engaged Oliver Baring, son of Esmond, to run the London end of Rowe & Pitman's Anglo American business. Baring had spent five years with Anglo American after Eton and McGill University. In 1974 he became a Rowe & Pitman partner – strangely, given the emphasis on family ties, the only son in the history of the firm to follow his father in this way.

Two years earlier the firm had strengthened the Johannesburg end of its business by setting up a local subsidiary, Rowe & Pitman (South Africa) Pty, with a brief to research South African industrial shares and service corporate clients in the Republic. Since Rowe & Pitman never hid the fact that it was the Anglo broker first and foremost, rival industrial groups were slow to rush to its colours. But, with Oppenheimer interests controlling 40 per cent of the Johannesburg stock exchange, nobody in London complained too much: there was plenty of business to be done. As an additional family link, Robin Wilson, nephew of

Comar Wilson, was hired to run the new office.

Europe, as always, was a special case. Peter Henderson had made the firm's first contacts there in the early 1950s, but it had been a salutary and often disheartening experience. He found continental businesses even more opaque than their British counterparts on matters of disclosure. As a result their shares were difficult to sell to UK investors. Conversely, European investors' obsession with yield made them unwilling to buy UK equities, where the standard rate of income tax was deducted from dividends at source.

Engaging personality though he was, Henderson was unable to make significant inroads into Europe. Big meetings terrified him so much that his hands would visibly shake. He drew strength from Ian Fleming, a Europhile who still attended the firm's lunches from time to time. Gradually he learned to sell blue-chip German shares such as Daimler Benz and Siemens to British investors, and he forged important institutional links, notably with Robeco, the Dutch investment group with the biggest open-ended fund in Europe. But his heart was never in such activities. For several years before retiring prematurely in 1968, he preferred to busy himself with duties on the Stock Exchange Council. He was spoken about as a future Chairman of the Exchange, but he opted to pursue more pleasurable country interests.

As a result Rowe & Pitman was slow to participate when Eurobonds took off in 1964. Henderson refused to allow the firm to make any sizeable market in the bonds because he felt this would have put the firm in the role of a jobber. Despite the odd fluke, like the time Ogilvy and Brooke bought bonds from Deutsche Bank in Frankfurt and sold them at a substantial profit to Deutsche Bank in Mannheim, the most frequently heard response to telephone enquiries to the Foreign Department was 'Sorry, the bond dealer's at lunch.' Rowe & Pitman's placing power in Eurobonds was therefore negligible. That did not stop Hambros faithfully trying to involve Rowe & Pitman as broker in one of its first Eurobond issues for Copenhagen Telephone. When Julian Martin Smith confessed to Jocelyn Hambro that the firm did not have the expertise, young James Ogilvy, who had cut his teeth in the Private Client Department, offered to help. He claimed to have learned about these new instruments from Will Hopper, a Eurobond expert at Warburg, who had impressed on him the importance of access to the top *banques privées* in Switzerland.

Ogilvy made an appointment to visit the most influential Swiss financier he knew, Paul Kern of Hambros Zurich, who he hoped would introduce him to the necessary, very desirable *banques privées*. (Hambros Zurich was a joint venture between Hambros Bank and Panmure Gordon which had been set up before the war to arrange sovereign issues.) Over lunch Kern quizzed the eager Ogilvy. 'My boy, do you speak German?' he asked. The answer was 'No'. 'Do you speak French?' Again, 'No'. 'And what is more you've got the wrong-shaped nose.'

Another time Ogilvy travelled to Switzerland to make a Eurobond sales pitch with Denis Milne, a close friend of Charles Hambro, who had recently joined Rowe & Pitman as a partner after a career as a Lloyd's broker. Sitting in a bank in Zurich, the two men were taken aback by the coolness of the reception they were receiving. Suddenly a grim-faced Ogilvy passed Milne a note, 'We're in the wrong bank. The potted plant is on the wrong side of the desk.'

Ogilvy had more luck a few years later in 1966 when he had a call from someone calling himself Henry Buhle III. 'I have been given your name,' he was told, 'and I'd like you to have some underwriting in IOS [International Overseas Securities].' When Ogilvy protested that he knew no one of that name, he was told not to worry: he had been allocated 5,000 shares at $10 each. At the time little had been heard of Bernie Cornfeld's International Overseas Securities. After making some enquiries, Ogilvy and David Brooke felt satisfied that this was an outfit they could do business with. They were helped by the discovery that the shares were trading on an 'on and if' basis of $13, or a full 30 per cent premium. However Julian Martin Smith, prompted particularly by Michael Bonsor, was reluctant to allow the firm to take the shares on offer. Ogilvy and Brooke consequently decided to take them for themselves. As the price rose, they noticed a discernible weakening from the other partners. Eventually Martin Smith summoned Ogilvy and told him he had decided to allow each partner a quota of 250 shares. The stock rose fourteen times the following year, netting each partner £15,000.

Shortly afterwards Ogilvy was passing the office where Denis Milne ran the Eurobond business. He heard Milne dismissing a very tall Dutchman with the uncharacteristically curt words, 'No, you can bloody well get it for yourself.' On his way out, the Dutchman bumped into Ogilvy and, when asked what had happened, said morosely that he had only asked for the register of Plessey shareholders. Taking pity, Ogilvy invited him out to lunch where he learned that his new friend was called Joe Melse and he ran the International Investment Trust (IIT), the open-ended mutual fund subsidiary of IOS.

The two men quickly struck up a business relationship. When Melse asked Ogilvy to deal for him, he said that all IIT funds were guaranteed by two top institutions, the Royal Trust Company of Canada and Credit Suisse. If anything ever looked like going wrong, he promised to inform Ogilvy straight away. So Ogilvy agreed to run a gold fund for Melse, as well as buying and selling all his UK equities. The IIT connection brought a vast and regular amount of business. 'It made Morgan Grenfell look tiny,' said Ogilvy. 'IOS soon represented 30 per cent of our turnover on a daily basis.' His own dealing books show that, if anything, this was an underestimate. In the depressed Operations Room, Ro Wadham bought a football rattle that he would twirl, making a fearful racket, every time a deal worth more than £250,000 (invariably from IIT or an associate) went through. However, given the volume of this business, the partners decided it would be wise to ignore IIT figures when it came to planning the firm's annual revenue and cost estimates.

Despite adverse comment, all went well for three more years until 1970 when Melse rang to tell Ogilvy that Credit Suisse was no longer acting as a trustee and that IIT funds were shortly to come under the care of the Overseas Development Bank, another IOS subsidiary operating out of Luxembourg. Realizing that something had gone wrong, Ogilvy alerted the Stock Exchange. Before long he received a call from Robert Vesco, who had taken over the helm of IOS from Bernie Cornfeld. 'I understand you're shitting me in London,' Vesco told Ogilvy. After further enquiries, Rowe & Pitman decided to cease trading for IOS. Some partners were reluctant to do this because the business was so profitable. Consequently Martin Smith and Bonsor, the original sceptics, went to see Vesco, and pronounced themselves satisfied. The next day IOS crashed, but not before Rowe & Pitman had reduced its exposure to next to nothing.

Amusing, chancy and profitable though the IIT connection had been, it only underlined an incontrovertible feature of City life – the growing purchasing power of various institutional funds, ranging from pension funds through unit trusts to American-style 'mutuals'. In response, Rowe & Pitman began to boost its own investment management side, leading to the setting up of a specialist fund management service in 1976. But before this happened, the firm still had to go through considerable internal upheaval.

7 New Broom

IN MARCH 1970 Rowe & Pitman changed it hours of work. Until then partners were supposed to be in their offices at 9.45, which often meant they weren't at their desks until ten o'clock. This, as Julian Martin Smith, the new Senior Partner acknowledged, was no longer acceptable in the bustling new City. 'It is becoming increasingly apparent in many ways that a 9.45 start, comfortable though it has been, is quite out of keeping with the spirit of the modern age, and we have had a good many comments from clients and others who have found difficulty in getting any sense out of Rowe & Pitman until after 9.45.' So, 'to bring us in line with the hours of our clients', Martin Smith introduced a new working schedule from 9.30 to 5.30.

Reaching the office a quarter of an hour earlier was hardly revolutionary, but it was symptomatic of important changes taking place in the partnership at the time. The long reign of Arthur Anderson as Senior Partner, followed by the two-year interregnum under the gentlemanly Tom Leveson Gower, had finally ended with the latter's retirement in April 1968.

Not everyone was convinced that Martin Smith had the 'right stuff' to lead the firm at the time. His overt habits of sucking on his pipe and keeping his mouth shut, only offering an opinion when it was absolutely necessary, seemed quaintly old fashioned. Often he would put his pipe into his pocket before deliberating, and, on at least one occasion, his suit caught fire. However, it did not take his colleagues long to realize that they had chosen correctly. Martin Smith was a wise man with an iron Hambro will who, while not abandoning tried and tested ways, was prepared to give younger partners their head.

Martin Smith's priority was to work out a strategy for Rowe & Pitman's future. There was no doubt the firm was one of the City of London's top brokers. But its growth during the 1960s had been haphazard, following the market into various situations (such as opening an American subsidiary) rather than leading it. Rowe & Pitman was well placed as an intermediary between the merchant banks and the institutions (with their growing array of funds). But market share in the core business of buying and selling stocks was static, and the banks were pressing for Rowe & Pitman to reduce its charges. How could the firm continue to grow in an environment where the globalization of the securities business was rather more than twinkle in visionaries' eyes?

One of Martin Smith's first moves in October 1968 was to call a weekend meeting of all seventeen partners in the luxury surroundings of the Compleat Angler Hotel in Marlow. The object was to thrash out where the firm was going, both in its own right and in relation to the rest of the market. With his usual conciseness, Bill Mackworth-Young later summarized the conclusions, as follows:

> (i) To get bigger, not to consolidate: and to achieve this aim by ourselves, not by amalgamation.
>
> (ii) To concentrate on our traditional business, i.e. broking UK stocks for UK institutions, while not closing our minds to expansion in other fields, particularly in R & P Inc. and in the Eurobond market.
>
> (iii) Accordingly, to enlarge considerably the Ops Room, the Gilt Edged department and the Research Department.
>
> (iv) To plan for sufficient dealing capacity, settlement capacity and office space for 500 bargains per day (versus 325 approx. in 1968), moving the office if necessary.

As Mackworth-Young implied, one of the problems holding Rowe & Pitman back was logistical. It had developed a Research

Department and set up an embryonic Operations Room. But the growing volume of business was already putting a considerable strain on both manpower and resources. When, that autumn, the Office Manager Con Rayment's health broke down and he asked to be allowed to retire, Martin Smith commissioned Nigel Elwes to write a report on Rowe & Pitman's settlement and accounting procedures, which were considered to be the worst bottle-neck holding the company back from making the most of its opportunities.

The situation was exacerbated by the changing requirements of the Stock Exchange. An example arose in the firm's turbulent relationship with Lord Beaverbrook. The 1963 Stock Transfer Act had introduced a new form of transfer that did not require the signature of the purchaser of the security. A few months later, however, this new system fell down when the Beaverbrook Foundation wanted to sell 1,400 shares in Beaverbrook Newspapers. Julian Martin Smith was forced to write Beaverbrook a grovelling letter, accepting partial responsibility for the problem. His client was not impressed, annotating the missive, 'I think the Stock Exchange is a quite contemptible body when it tries to renege on a mistake made at our expense, and to our discomfort. . . . It's time the Stock Exchange was realising the very big commissions that are paid to them and they are expected for that payment to render a service to the public.'

In attempting to address the general bureaucratic impasse, the financially astute Elwes noted tactfully that 'the present material sent to clients from the Settlements Department in the form of statements etc. is not very neat and could easily lead to an impression of inefficiency'. He made clear that the firm would have to grasp a nettle it had avoided and invest in computerization. (This had been viewed askance by some of the partners who feared the capital outlays required.) Elwes also pointed out that the existing problems had been aggravated by the number of small bargains that had to be processed. While acknowledging that some of this business (largely from the banks) was unavoidable, he challengingly suggested that Rowe & Pitman should encourage its private clients, 'particularly with portfolios of up to about £50,000', to switch their holdings to newly established Rowe & Pitman funds such as unit trusts.

The following month Martin Smith announced a shake-up of the general or back office. Rayment was to retire, and in his stead Arthur Little, son of Harry, the original Partnership Manager, was to be made a partner with overall responsibility for administration, which included all settlements. As day-to-day Office Manager, Martin Smith appointed Peter Smith (this time no relation) with the assistance of Douglas Carson. Without specifying any dates, he promised to replace 'the old iron' under which the department laboured with 'more modern forms of machinery'.

It was Arthur Little who, once upon a time, had been prevented from joining the firm because he was an Old Olavian. He was the third Rowe & Pitman clerk to 'rise from the ranks' to the partnership. Bill Corney had been the first in 1965, followed by Alan Davenport, the new head of the Operations Room, earlier in 1968. As well as advising all partners on technical aspects of Stock Exchange practice, Corney now ran virtually his own operation – ensuring the smooth passage of new issues, which meant everything from writing prospectuses to ironing out any difficulties with the Exchange's Quotations Committee.

The Mackworth-Young memo referred to expanding the Operations Rooms, the Gilt-edged Department and the Research Department. With its excellent grounding by Jim Graham Watson, the last of these could, under the able D'Albiac, more than hold its own in the ensuing battle for corporate resources. The other two were more problematic.

The Operations Room was starting to evolve as the centre for the co-ordination of institutional sales. But it made slow progress at first because it was too diverse, and therefore unable to match market information from the Research Department with the needs of the institutional salesmen, gilts traders and fund managers. Nominally the Operations Room was under the benign control of Alan Davenport, a graduate of Edinburgh University who had worked as a gilts researcher. But the salesmen – the young bloods who were supposed to win Rowe & Pitman more of its traditional broking business – felt they were not giving an adequate service. A survey in the early 1970s showed that, out of the firm's 248 institutional clients, only 111 were fully covered, 48 were adequately covered, 55 were inadequately covered and 34 were not covered at all.

Unease at this situation was articulated in an August 1972 memo from James D'Albiac who stated baldly that 'the ops rooms is one of our most inefficient departments' because it was attempting to serve two masters – Davenport, its day-to-day head, and Wilmot-Sitwell, who ran the sales force responsible for distributing the corporate products on behalf of the merchant banks and who had direct access to senior partners. Neither of these two principals 'feels the obligation/responsibility/pressure to ruthlessly examine ops room lists for evidence of adequate service', wrote D'Albiac. 'Perhaps each feels inhibited by an uncertainty with regard to the other.'

At a higher level than Wilmot-Sitwell, the partner spearheading the drive for increasing business was Bill Mackworth-Young who, in advance of the pack, had developed into a corporate broker par excellence. Mackworth-Young was the partner with the closest links to the merchant banks, who admired his fine sense of the market. Indeed, following the retirement of Sir Antony Hornby as Cazenove's senior partner in 1970, no broker could rival him. His pricing of a new issue was so precise that a merchant bank head like Kenneth Keith of Hill Samuel would summon him to comment on the efforts of his competitors.

Mackworth-Young's work on new issues had convinced him that Rowe & Pitman should resist the temptation to go the way of Helbert Wagg in the 1920s. It should not compete directly with the merchant banks by becoming an issuing house in its own right. Rather Rowe & Pitman should concentrate on developing services which were complementary to the merchant banks, while going all out for a larger share of the available UK equity and fixed-interest stockbroking business.

With his wide experience Mackworth-Young was more upbeat than some of his colleagues about the Operations Room. He felt it had 'in fact done a very good job indeed, generating and handling a greater volume of business and a wider spread of busi-

THE FOUNDERS

George Rowe

Fred Pitman

Lancy Hugh Smith's XI at Mount Clare 1912. Lancy Hugh Smith is seated in the centre, with Harry Little on his left (our right). In the centre of the back row, behind Lancy Hugh Smith, with white hair, is Tommy Britton, the office manager, and on his left (our right) is W.T. Craven

Cricket at Titsey Place in the early 1950s. The front row includes Wilfred de Knoop (second from left), Hilary Bray (third from left) and Constant Rayment (second from right)

Lancy Hugh Smith

Hugo Pitman

Fitz Graham Watson

Arthur Anderson

Smith and Nephew: Julian Martin Smith (left) and Nigel Elwes

Baring and Son: Esmond Baring (left) and Oliver Baring

Nick Verey presents Peter Wilmot-Sitwell with an Augustus John portrait of Hugo Pitman on his retirement

Queen Elizabeth the Queen Mother visits Woolgate House, November 1971. Also in picture: Bill Mackworth Young (second from left), James Ogilvy (partially obscured, third from left), Peter Vanneck (third from left) and Julian Martin Smith (second from right)

Denis Milne

David Innes

Alan Hurst Brown

Ian Fleming

Peter Wilmot-Sitwell

James Ogilvy

David Brooke

James D'Albiac

Signing an agreement with J. Sainsbury

The Operations Room in the mid-1970s

ness than ever before. Moreover if the Ops Room had expanded faster before now it might well have lost the cohesive team spirit which is one of its strongest qualities.' His parody of Kipling's poem 'If' further raised morale, with its brilliant evocation of the sterling qualities required by a stockbroker in the modern City.

Gilts remained the Cinderella of the partnership at this stage. Within the London market as a whole they accounted for roughly three-quarters of turnover. But Rowe & Pitman devoted little thought to their development, apart from initiating a dedicated research team (initially, Alan Davenport and Jim Martin), which provided institutional customers with up-to-date statistics, and a review service, run by Tom Ferguson and Clive Haynes, which compiled quarterly, semi-annual and annual valuations for important clients. As a result the Rowe & Pitman Gilts Department ticked over with 1,190 personal portfolios, worth £55 million in 1967. But the firm's market share was falling – down from 1.13 per cent of total Stock Exchange turnover in 1964 to 0.67 per cent in 1968.

In this situation David Innes, head of the Gilts Department, peppered the partners with proposals for further expansion. In the wake of the Marlow conference, he gained an assistant in Michael Franzman and then in March 1969 a second partner in the form of Geoffrey Finn, a gilts specialist who had worked for Joseph Sebag and W.I. Carr. Subsequently Tony Radcliffe and Richard Rhodes joined the team – both, like Franzman and Finn, later becoming partners in their own right. These moves had an immediate effect, as in 1969, Rowe & Pitman's gilts turnover quadrupled, giving it over 2 per cent of the Stock Exchange total. Over the six years from 1965 to 1971 total gilt-edged dealing commission rose in line from £49,002 to £307,714.

Always quick to break into verse if an opportunity arose, Bill Mackworth-Young celebrated the issue of Conversion 3½% Stock 1969 – which, unusually for those days, had a single conversion date – with a ditty entitled 'The Bond-Boy's Girl-Friend':

> Some dealers sigh for Transport,
> Or swear that Gas is heaven;
> And some have younger mistresses
> Like Funding '57.
> But all these tawdry harlots
> Are no affair of mine -
> My heart is set upon my pet
> Conversion '69.
>
> Eternity is far too old;
> Consols are rather worn.
> And War Loan's somewhat ageless,
> And Victory looks drawn.
> So I embrace Conversion
> And then, with trembling nerves,
> Investigate her single date
> And feel her yielding curves.
>
> For though she came out recently
> She has no sense of shame;
> She goes to bed with Bankers -
> But I love her just the same.
> She's more than gilt – she's golden,
> And I, her humble serf,
> Adore the wench because, in French,
> Her name is 'Soixante-Neuf'.

By November 1973, Innes could reflect contentedly about Rowe & Pitman's gilts business, 'The client spread is now reasonably wide. Although the National Westminster Bank, and funds under their management, accounts for a very significant and certainly the largest slice of total commissions, this is at least a quality customer.' Five years later, in 1978, his department was earning more commission from gilts in one day than in the whole of the year 1958. After the abolition of exchange controls in October 1979, Rowe & Pitman acted as broker to roughly three-quarters of all fixed-rate sterling 'Bulldog' issues, playing an important role in the development of both primary and secondary markets for these instruments. 'Bulldogs' were particularly active between 1980 and 1982 when there was a temporary downturn in equities, and their success helped raise Rowe & Pitman's profile with international banks at a crucial moment in the globalization of finance.

Recognition of Rowe & Pitman's increasing stature in the marketing of government stocks came in July 1972 when the Bank of England appointed the firm one of its six recognized money brokers on the Stock Exchange. Under the overall direction of Innes, this new side of the business proved a success, particularly after Peter Morley came from Clive Discount as Managing Director of the firm's new subsidiary, Rowe & Pitman Money Broking, with the status of partner from 1974.

Changes even took place on the floor of the Stock Exchange, where Rowe & Pitman had begun to appoint a series of dealing partners. In the early 1960s, David Innes used to be found in the 'box', where he liked to do his own dealing in gilts. He was joined by William Robson who, for a period, overlooked the firm's equity dealings. In the mid-1960s, this position was institutionalized with the appointment of Timmy Gibbs as Rowe & Pitman's first Market Partner. The Old Etonian Gibbs had few natural abilities as a stockbroker, but he was liked by the dealing staff and, as far as the partnership was concerned, he had the advantage of being a stepson of Lord Harcourt, who succeeded Lord Bicester as Chairman of Morgan Grenfell. After Gibbs's retirement in 1975, he was followed as Market Partner by Peter Heming Johnson, who had been introduced to the firm in the mid-1950s through a connection with the Leveson Gower family. (Heming Johnson had to wait until 1977 for his appointment, since there was a moratorium on making new partners after the RHB merger in 1975.)

Heming Johnson's pay as a clerk in the transfer department in 1956 had been £5 a week, which sufficed at a time when a good lunch at Lyons in Throgmorton Street could be had for 3s 1d. After National Service, he returned to the firm in 1959 on the slightly increased salary of £330 a year. After a further year in the

Transfer Department, he made his way onto the floor of the Stock Exchange, where his initial responsibilities as a 'blue button' were to take telephone calls and keep the prices in the dealing box up to date. After four years as a blue button, he became an official dealer, where his main task, together with Cyril Cook, was servicing the twenty or so provincial stockbrokers who dealt through Rowe & Pitman. (At the time the relationship with William F. Coates in Belfast and Penny McGeorge in Glasgow was particularly strong.)

In the early 1960s the much respected Senior Dealer was Teddy Downer, who followed in the footsteps of the redoubtable Fred Jay. (Lionel Fraser, chairman of Helbert Wagg, used to call him directly, saying he always learned more about the state of the market from Downer than from any partner.) Downer was assisted (and later succeeded) by John Ramsay, who carved out a niche as the king of the South African mining ('Kaffir') market. Ramsay made way for Jack Gaymer as senior dealer, and his responsibility for 'Kaffirs' passed to Jim Finch. Other notable dealers during this period were Chris Andrews, Joe Walker and Harold Wimpress, who specialized in fixed-interest securities. These men, supplemented later by Philip Ellick, formed the nucleus of the remarkable team of dealers which executed the dawn raids of the late 1970s and early 1980s. They were kept in order by Miss Bates, the 'box' telephonist who was known throughout the City for her no-nonsense manner.

With an expanded back office, Operations Room, Gilts and New Issues Department, not to mention a hugely developed fund management operation, space at Rowe & Pitman suddenly became seriously at a premium – as indeed had been recognized at the 1968 Marlow conference. Temporary salvation came in 1970 when the Bucklersbury House lease was sold, and a more substantial (and comfortable) premises was acquired in Woolgate House, a new office block in Coleman Street on the east side of Guildhall – albeit at a price of £9 per square foot (which was partly offset by renting an unused section to Cazenove).

Through Alan Walsh, a clerk who combined compiling crosswords for *The Times* with good connections at the Post Office,

Rowe & Pitman acquired the telephone number MONarch 1066 (before long 606 1066) which, while jokingly alluding to the firm's supposed royal connections, had the advantage of being genuinely memorable. But, although this number was jealously guarded thenceforth, the business did not remain long at Woolgate House. For in 1973 an office property boom began to stoke up. During the course of the year, the partners were approached by Chase Manhattan, who occupied part of the building and wanted to take it over entirely. This offer came at a time when Rowe & Pitman was experiencing unprecedented cash-flow difficulties – the result of greater than ever partnership expenses, coupled with continued bottle-necks in the back office.

Denis Milne had moved from selling gilts and Eurobonds, which was not his forte, to becoming a successful corporate broker, developing strong ties with Rentokil, Sainsbury and Plessey. Milne noticed that many middle-range companies, particularly in the Midlands, avoided the City because, as he put it, 'they were afraid of getting their trousers taken off'. Plessey was an example: 'Nobody had been to see them for ages. As I used to come across John Clark [the Plessey Chief Executive Officer from 1962 to 1989] outside the City, I made it my business to get to know them better.'

Known for his poker-playing ability, Milne now offered to take charge of the Woolgate House negotiations with Chase. He headed a Rowe & Pitman team which also comprised David Innes, Arthur Little and David King, an estates consultant. After his first talks he returned to the partners with the news that they were being offered £20 per square foot. To some younger members struggling to pay increased partnership shares, this seemed like a very welcome recapitalization of their business. But Milne told them it was not enough. With twenty-five years of its thirty-year lease remaining, and with a ten-year break clause instead of the usual five years, he felt Rowe & Pitman was in a strong position to bargain for more. Since another bidder had emerged in Hammerson Property Group, the building's landlords, he decided to hold a tender, with these two companies submitting their bids in sealed envelopes. Mouths dropped when the first envelope was opened and Hammerson had decided to drop out. Better news awaited them in the second, which contained Chase's offer at the equivalent of £32 per square foot.

Again Milne was not satisfied and thought he could obtain more. At this stage James Ogilvy was deputed to approach Julian Martin Smith on behalf of several financially overextended junior partners and let him know that they felt this was madness. After going through his well-known pipe-filling ritual, the Senior Partner dismissed the threat of insurrection and decided to let Milne go ahead. At the conclusion of one further round of negotiations, Chase had increased its offer to an incredible £42 per square foot and agreed to allow Rowe & Pitman unlimited time to seek new premises. The agitated junior members were relieved to find that this whole process had brought a windfall in the shape of a £3 million capital injection into the partnership.

Looking for new accommodation in an over-heated property market was not easy. Eventually Rowe & Pitman had to compromise, splitting its partners and staff between two offices, the Investment Management Department in City Gate House on Finsbury Square and the money brokers, institutional salesmen and corporate financiers on the sixteenth floor of the Stock Exchange Tower, where they revelled in their proximity to events on the main dealing floor beneath them.

Even then the saga of this particular move was not over. After Chase Manhattan had managed to introduce a term clause into its purchase agreement, Rowe & Pitman was required to leave Woolgate House by December 1974. However a week before this date, they learned that their moving firm had gone on strike. Mindful that their lawyer had impressed on them the need to give Chase vacant possession (otherwise it might renege on the deal), a team of partners and staff went to the offices over the weekend and moved the fixtures and fittings to their new premises. The day before they officially quit, their lawyer came to visit a now virtually empty Woolgate House. Again he was not satisfied: they had not provided vacant possession, he said, because they had neglected to remove the battery of telephones. Hastily a tip was hired, the windows were opened, and during one lunch hour over 1,000 telephones were hurled into the street.

While at Woolgate House Rowe & Pitman had started a sport and social club in a dedicated room, with facilities for table games and darts, on the eighth floor. Befitting a firm which harks back to a couple of enthusiastic oarsmen, this emphasized the importance attached within Rowe & Pitman to extra-curricular and, in particular, sporting, activities.

The sport that brought everyone in the firm together, from the grandest partner to the lowliest office boy, was undoubtedly cricket. In August 1912 Lancy began hosting a series of lavish summer garden parties at Mount Clare, Roehampton, where the day-long proceedings were dominated by a cricket match – in this first case, between two teams of thirteen a side, captained by Lancy himself and by his nephew Julian Martin Smith. On both this occasion and in 1913, Martin Smith's team won handsomely. No further cricket games were played until 1922 when the staff was invited to Jock Bowes-Lyon's house at St Paul's Waldenbury, near Hitchin in Hertfordshire, where a Rowe & Pitman team was soundly thrashed by the local village side. These fixtures, which continued until 1929, shortly before Bowes-Lyon's death, were often attended by his sister, the Duchess of York, as the Hon. Lady Elizabeth Bowes-Lyon became after her marriage in April 1923. On one of these occasions, it is reported, some female staff members insisted that Bowes-Lyon show them the spot where the Duke of York had proposed to his sister.

The following decade Lancy began inviting staff to his newly acquired seat at the Old Hall, Garboldisham, in Suffolk, where Rowe & Pitman played a side made up from his domestic staff. In 1937, Bill Palmer steered Rowe & Pitman to victory with a magnificent unbeaten century – a feat Lancy commemorated by giving the Office Manager an inscribed silver mug, with strict instructions never to drink his beer from anything else.

On his death in 1941, Lancelot Hugh Smith left Garboldisham to Esmond Baring, who revived the fixture after the war – both there and at Abbotsworthy House, his own family estate at

Kingsworthy, near Winchester. With his cricketing connections (his uncle Sir Henry Leveson Gower, known as 'Shrimp', had been President of Surrey County Cricket Club and a Test selector), Tom Leveson Gower enjoyed the game and invited the staff to play at his house, Titsey Place, in the early 1950s. Later on, the nature of the fixture varied, with the partners taking on the staff, or with those working in City Gate House challenging their colleagues in the Stock Exchange Tower. Various local rules applied, the most important being not to get the Senior Partner out too early.

Over the years, the firm has been able to call on the services of several excellent players. Herbert Benka, a clerk, was a gifted middle-order right-hand batsman and slow left-arm bowler who played eleven matches for Middlesex between 1933 and 1936. Errol Holmes, an 'orchid' whose father had been advised by Sir David Yule that Rowe & Pitman was the only worthwhile place of employment for his son, saw action as a hard-hitting batsman and useful fast bowler. With an Oxford blue in both soccer and cricket, he played for Surrey between 1924 and 1955, captaining the county from 1934 to 1938, and again in 1947 and 1948. After touring with the MCC to Jamaica in 1926/7 and the West Indies in 1934/5, he led the team in Australia and New Zealand in 1935/6. More recently, the appositely named Charles Rowe, a UK equity salesman, played for Kent. With Will Robins, a UK equity analyst, (son of R.V.C. Robins, the former Middlesex county cricketer, and grandson of Walter Robins, the England captain), he helped guide the Rowe & Pitman team to success in the Stock Exchange cricket cup in 1984 and 1985.

Following in the St Olave's tradition, football also featured prominently on the Rowe & Pitman sporting calendar. The soccer team played its matches on grounds (subsidized by the firm) in Lower Sydenham and subsequently Preston Road, Wembley. At first Rowe & Pitman fielded its own side, later combining with Gordon Askew & Biddulph and then with Linton Clarke and Company, with whom it once reached the final of the Combination Cup, only to lose by a single goal in extra time. A team stalwart was the centre half, Teddy Downer, who also played for the Norsemen, a famous amateur eleven of that period. An outstanding natural player, he was regularly picked for the Stock Exchange in their representative games with the Liverpool and Paris Exchanges.

Rowe & Pitman's overall sporting prowess was not so obvious in post-war years, although as late as November 1974 it won the Stock Exchange cross-country championship on Wimbledon Common, with two members of the staff, C. West and R. Silk taking second and third places in the individual competition.

In addition, the firm participated in a wide range of minor sports. When the jingoistic mood surrounding the Boer War and the run-up to the First World War prompted a rash of rifle clubs throughout the country, Rowe & Pitman – not to be outdone in demonstrating its patriotism – formed its own Remigium Rifle Club and with the appropriate motto *Recte Occulo Recte Animo* ('rightly with the eye, rightly with the mind', or more colloquially, 'good shot, good chap'.) The club operated on a miniature range at the Lavington Street Baths in Southwark, before moving to a more convenient location under the arches at Broad Street Station. With the help of loans from the firm, club members were encouraged to purchase their own rifles. In their annual competition for the silver gilt cup presented by George Rowe, John Longden, from the Name Department, who was wounded in 1915 serving with the Honourable Artillery Company, consistently proved the best shot, with A.J. Battie of the Transfer Section a close second. The Club Secretary was Edward Collier, who opted not to return to Rowe & Pitman after being wounded as a second lieutenant with the Devon Regiment.

Following the war, bullets were beaten into darts, arguably a more sociable activity. Dating from the 1920s, the Rowe & Pitman darts team joined the Stock Exchange Darts League. Games were usually played in City pubs, but on special occasions 43 Bishopsgate was used as a venue. Special permission had to be granted to keep a barrel of beer in the office, provided it was kept out of sight during the day. When the list of fixtures was expanded to include firms outside the Stock Exchange, Ian Fleming presented a trophy known as the Silver Dart, whose last known winner was Glyn Mills. At Woolgate House, with its games room, table tennis became so strongly competitive that Geoffrey Finn and Denis Milne presented two cups, the former for the men, the latter for the ladies.

The partners, meanwhile, had their own well-established routines of mixing business with sporting pleasure. It would be interesting to chart the contribution that the grouse moor and the golf course made to either their general well-being or the firm's bottom line, but unfortunately records are not available. Several excellent golfers passed through the partnership including Hugh Vivian Smith, Ian Fleming, Hilary Bray (a former blue) and Denis Milne. More esoterically, Bill Mackworth-Young liked to fly a glider (though in July 1956 he had to suffer the ignominy of the newspapers reporting that he had been forced to land his glider in Horsham Park in Sussex, while flying to visit the Hendersons in Storrington). Thirteen years later Peter Heming Johnson initiated the first of the now annual contests between the Stock Exchange Ski Club, which he helped found, and the Paris Bourse. His sixteen-man party in Val D'Isere in April 1969 included Rowe & Pitman stalwarts Sir Peter Vanneck, Richard Bonsor and Alan Bulmer, himself a grandson of Arthur Anderson.

Less heartily, but equally sociably, Lancy Hugh Smith started the agreeable custom of inviting staff members to dinner with the partners in a specially erected marquee at Mount Clare. After the meal there was often an entertainment: on one occasion, to everyone's amusement, Fred Pitman lost his braces to a skilful magician. These staff dinners were continued later in annual dinners at the Connaught and Whitbread Rooms (where the comedian's racy patter was not to everyone's taste) and the Rembrandt, Hilton, Dorchester and Grosvenor House hotels. Latterly Rowe & Pitman's social tradition has been maintained in the regular buffet luncheon for retired partners and staff.

No reference to culinary habits would be complete without

mentioning the partners' lunches. Despite Lancy's temporary restrictions on port in the 1930s, these tended to be convivial affairs. While at Bishopsgate, Hambros provided the meal, which was rated adequate but not as good as the fare at Hoare's Bank or the Anglo American Corporation. When Rowe & Pitman branched out on its own at Bucklersbury House, its first cook was Maria Noble, daughter of a senior Conservative politician in Scotland. Subsequently, Annie Evill took charge of the partners' dining room at Woolgate House and City Gate House.

Apart from a succession of 'suits', visitors ranged from Margaret Thatcher and Enoch Powell to Eric Morecambe to Dickie Henderson (both of whom signed autographs for the women in the telephone exchange). Powell boosted morale by telling assembled partners how important they all were: 'I only stand up and talk in the House of Commons. But you take what I say and interpret it for the rest of the world. You are the greatest distributors of news that I know.'

Royal visitors included Princess Margaret and Diana, Princess of Wales. Perhaps most widely and most fondly remembered, however, was the Queen Mother. She first came as Duchess of York in the early 1930s, when she made a special point of contacting Mrs Craigie, the Hambros cook, who was known to her. Knight, a Cockney messenger who was pulled into service as a waiter for the day, made his name by telling her to 'mind yer 'ands, 'cos the plate is bloody 'ot'.

Over the years she returned on several occasions. In November 1971, during the firm's short stay at Woolgate House, she was proudly escorted round the premises by Julian Martin Smith, the Senior Partner, who introduced her – inter alia – to Bill Palmer, the former Office Manager, Peter Smith, his successor, and Joan Weaver, the formidable partners' secretary. A dozen years later, shortly before Rowe & Pitman's merger with S.G. Warburg, she came to lunch again – this time accompanied by her lady-in-waiting Lady Jean Rankin, whose son Sir Alick Rankin was Chairman of Scottish and Newcastle Breweries, a much-valued client of the firm and a childhood friend of several of the senior partners. These now pillars of the establishment had to endure considerable teasing as both these grand old ladies remembered them as young boys.

8 Searching for Partners

BILL MACKWORTH-YOUNG was famous for his crystal-ball gazing as well as poetry. In one of his regular exercises at peering into the future in February 1972, he was adamant: 'For some mystical reason which eludes us, Rowe & Pitman has a distinctive and advantageous "image" in the City, even among those merchant banks and other institutions who are not, in a real sense, our clients. Any amalgamation of importance would dilute this "image" and is therefore undesirable, unless as a lifeline in emergency.' Yet three years later Rowe & Pitman had given up its valued independent status and had merged with the established stockbroking firm Read Hurst-Brown. What is more, Mackworth-Young had left stockbroking for a new career as a merchant banker with Morgan Grenfell.

The two events were unrelated, but indicative of generally turbulent times. Mackworth-Young's departure – to deal with marginally the lesser matter – came after his keen sense of what was happening in the market made him press remorselessly for managerial changes. Part of the impetus had come from the Stock Exchange which now required each member firm to designate not only its senior partner but also its partners responsible for administration, finance and dealing. Together with the introduction of Ariel, a new semi-computerized settlement system, this only exacerbated the administrative problems at Rowe & Pitman, culminating in cash-flow difficulties that could no longer be ignored.

With over a dozen partners, the firm's direction was clearly becoming unwieldy. Its response in June 1971 was to form a new Executive Committee of five partners headed by Denis Milne. (An earlier, smaller Executive Committee had been mooted at the 1968 Marlow conference but had failed to get off the ground.) One of Milne's first moves in his new post was to send everyone in the firm a copy of Robert Townsend's *Up the Organization*, an early management textbook which humorously advocated an aggressive team approach to business. His Executive Committee spawned a Forward Planning Group – officially designed 'as a voice for the younger members of Rowe & Pitman' (or, as one of their number put, 'as a place for the hot-heads to let off steam'). In fact, it was hungrily seized upon by Mackworth-Young, its Chairman, to develop ideas about Rowe & Pitman's future.

An immediate problem recognized by the Group was that, for all its name, the Executive Committee lacked decision-making powers. Mackworth-Young therefore proposed to abolish this body and set up a Board of Management, with the Senior Partner as Chairman and with a fully fledged Secretary who would attend to all the partnership's affairs in a world of increasing bureaucracy. Formed on 1 January 1974, the first Board of Management consisted of Julian Martin Smith, the chairman, plus Ro Wadham, David Innes, Peter Wilmot-Sitwell, Denis Milne, James Ogilvy, Alan Davenport and Nigel Elwes. As its Secretary, the new Board drafted in John Lewington, an unassuming former Cambridge soccer blue, who had worked in investment research. Thenceforward, the Board met fortnightly, assuming responsibility for day-to-day policy and administration. Major decisions, particularly financial ones, were referred to the whole partnership, which continued to meet every quarter. In keeping with the new mood, Rowe & Pitman decided for the first time in its history to employ a public relations company. Charles Barker, the new consultants, recommended, along with obligatory changes in logos and letterheads, that the firm should be known by its acronym, R. & P., partly as a branding exercise, and partly to distinguish it from a couple of other City entities with similar names.

These managerial changes were Mackworth-Young's swan

Searching for Partners

song at Rowe & Pitman, for in the autumn of 1973 he requested three months' sabbatical leave. He went to Barrs, his much-loved estate on the west coast of Argyll which had become part of the Rowe & Pitman patrimony (Arthur Anderson, its original owner, left it to his nephew Hilary Bray, who in turn shared it with and later passed it on to Bill Mackworth-Young). When he returned in December 1973 ('exhausted but completely refreshed', as Julian Martin Smith once observed of his colleague's state of being after trips to Scotland), he announced to his astonished fellow partners that he intended to resign and join Morgan Grenfell, where his cousin John Stevens was Managing Director. Even the phlegmatic Julian Martin Smith found it difficult to hide his intense disappointment at the defection of the man he had personally seen as his eventual successor.

Ironically Mackworth-Young had opposed any dilution of the Rowe & Pitman name. Indeed, according to one partner, the strategy of growth without amalgamation had been 'set in stone'. But this attitude had been struck without advance knowledge of the four-fold oil price rise which came in the wake of the October 1973 Arab-Israel war and which led the following year to the stock market's worst downturn since the great crash of the early 1930s. This painful experience, coming on top of Rowe & Pitman's own problems of administration and cash-flow, convinced the partnership that it needed to take drastic measures.

One approach was to make a substantial (up to 50 per cent) cut in staff. The other was to look again at the possibility of expansion through a link with another firm, thus improving Rowe & Pitman's own capital base and range of services. According to one partner the overall picture was so bleak that the firm had no option but to go forward. Luckily the small team, comprising Nigel Elwes, Alan Davenport, James D'Albiac and Nick Verey, which was charged with re-examining the issue, managed to perform a nimble volte-face and opt unequivocally for some form of takeover, sooner rather than later.

Finding a partner for an established firm like Rowe & Pitman was not easy. Most other stockbrokers were hurting badly (or perhaps even worse – Rowe & Pitman was buoyed by its gold

111

share business, which provided a flicker of light in the general gloom). One suggestion was to link up with Sebags, which had occupied offices a few floors above Rowe & Pitman in Bucklersbury House. Another was to return to Read Hurst-Brown, a medium-sized firm with an excellent reputation, which had been sharply rebuffed when it had approached Rowe & Pitman a year earlier.

Read Hurst-Brown (RHB) was formed through the post-war amalgamation of two established firms, Read & Brigstock, and Hurst-Brown, Buckmaster & Peter Hicks. If Rowe & Pitman was a rowing establishment, RHB was known for the quality of its golfing partners, including Edward Bromley-Davenport and 'Ham' Martin, who had played for England, George Loveday (who was the then Chairman of the Stock Exchange) and Tommy Whitaker, who were both pre-war university blues, and John Littlewood, who, as Oxford University's captain, was recruited for the firm on the basis of a round of golf with Bromley-Davenport and Martin. (Other notable partners at RHB included Sir Edmund Stockdale, who had been Lord Mayor of London, and Derek Moore-Brabazon, son of the famous aviator and politician.)

More to the point, professionally, RHB had grown into a profitable niche stockbroker by trading on its detailed research into the property and insurance industries. In the absence of reliable information about property, RHB built up its own register of the holdings of quoted companies. From this it was able to make reliable estimates of asset values, the main influence on the share price of property companies. It also developed excellent contacts with the property industry. The RHB property team was led by Alastair Fergusson, a product of Winchester and Oxford, who came to the firm from Helbert Wagg and became a partner in 1961. Rather different in background was his right-hand man, Peter Hardy who, having joined the messengers' department as a 15-year-old school-leaver, had risen through the ranks and become a partner in 1967.

The insurance specialization was developed in the 1950s by Ham Martin, who joined the firm in 1953 from David A. Bevan to develop a small gilt-edged switching business. His instinctive mathematical skills led him to sense similar switching opportunities between the shares of insurance companies, whose business was not dissimilar and whose accounts were difficult to understand. Despite competition from Savory and Greenwell, RHB quickly made its mark with its annual publication of detailed statistics about insurance companies. In 1959 John Littlewood joined this team as RHB's first graduate trainee. He worked initially as an investment analyst, becoming a partner in 1964, and taking over the leadership when Martin retired in 1972.

In the early 1960s RHB's business was broadly spread with around 45 per cent of commission revenue coming from institutions, 45 per cent from private clients and 10 per cent from branch banks. The overall direction of the firm changed decisively in 1964 with the appointment of Alan Hurst-Brown as Senior Partner at the relatively young age of forty-three. Himself the son of a former Senior Partner (between 1957 and 1960), Hurst-Brown had spent his formative years at Wellington College, and in North Africa during the Second World War. Under his leadership RHB turned its attention more specifically to institutional business. A business downturn in 1966 led to some culling of unprofitable bank business, while other innovations included the creation of a Private Client Department and the launch of an in-house unit trust, the Merlin Fund.

RHB's reputation for specialist research served it well in the early 1970s. Its commission income exceeded £1 million for the first time in 1971 and, unlike most of its rivals, it even enjoyed a successful year in 1974 – partly by pruning its staff, and partly by advising on just about the only big takeover of any consequence that year, the Kuwait Investment Office's bid for St Martin's Property Corporation.

But the lease on RHB's office at 7 Birchin Lane was coming to an end and it could not afford the increase demanded by its landlord, Land Securities. In addition, several partners who had joined after the war were about to retire. When Alan Hurst-Brown sought advice from Ashley Ponsonby of Schroders, the firm's best client over the years, he was pointed in the direction of Rowe &

Pitman. But at that stage Julian Martin Smith told him categorically that he was not interested in a merger. RHB subsequently received approaches from Laing & Cruickshank and from Messel, but felt neither was profitable enough to make a link worthwhile.

Meanwhile Rowe & Pitman was hurting badly from the effects of the market downturn. In Woolgate House's Room 3, where junior partners not otherwise engaged in entertaining clients would meet to eat their sandwiches, a spirit of gloom pervaded. Normally Room 3 was considered the epicentre for constructive radicalism, as shown by D'Albiac, Elwes and others. Now, as the stock market plunged, these Young Turks became seriously concerned about their often highly mortgaged futures. (Several had borrowed substantially to finance their partnerships, though they were eligible for special mortgage facilities from Hoare and Company.)

When Rowe & Pitman began to reconsider RHB's approach, James Ogilvy was deputed to make the initial contact because he had worked with Alan Taylor, the partner who ran the latter firm's Private Client Department. He found RHB on the brink of signing a contract for new premises. This meant that discussions moved extremely quickly from then on. Negotiations between Ogilvy and Nigel Elwes for Rowe & Pitman, and John Littlewood and Alastair Fergusson for RHB began on 26 November 1974 and were concluded less than a month later on 20 December. At the time Rowe & Pitman had twenty-five partners (all capital), while RHB had twenty-two (of whom sixteen were capital). In round terms Rowe & Pitman's revenues were 2.6 times those of RHB, but its expenses were higher at 2.9 times. Rowe & Pitman's revenues were more broadly based and drawn from gilts, equities (both domestic and overseas), corporate finance and money broking. RHB's revenues were drawn almost entirely from UK equities, where it had a 1 per cent market share, compared with Rowe & Pitman's 1.8 per cent.

Rowe & Pitman wanted the new firm to have thirty partners, out of which it would provide twenty-two and RHB eight. While this proved acceptable, Rowe & Pitman's proposal for an 80:20 equity split was not, and had to be renegotiated at 77.5:22.5

(and 6:2 on the Board of Management). The resulting merger was announced to the world on Friday, 3 January 1975, one business day before the FT Index touched its notorious low point of 146, and the new firm opened for business three months later, in April. Initially it was known as Rowe & Pitman Hurst-Brown, a form that was religiously adhered to until April 1979 when the urbane Alan Hurst-Brown became Senior Partner and, having no desire to trumpet his own name, was quite happy for the more succinct 'Rowe & Pitman' to be used officially again.

It was, by all accounts, a happy and fruitful liaison from the start – a fact that was recognized when, at a cost of £25,000, each staff member was awarded an *ex gratia* payment of £100. As the mathematics indicate, Rowe & Pitman now employed 250 staff, a figure which remained fairly static, give or take 20 people, until 1982, when the 300 mark was passed. The 'old' Rowe & Pitman had in fact comfortably exceeded this figure in 1973 when it employed 350 people. At the same time RHB had 140 staff. These numbers had been significantly cut back during the bad days of 1974. Now the overlapping settlement and support teams allowed scope for further reductions.

If the new faces were a little difficult to recognize (and track down), the telephonists knew how to deal with the situation. In May, Anne Pile, Thelma Joel, Janice Wingfield and Barbara Alpe, the four women in the office exchange, penned a poem to the partners, who were proving particularly elusive.

> *This is a plea, to our partners dear*
> *Sit up straight and lend an ear.*
>
> *We seek them here, we seek them there,*
> *We seek those partners everywhere.*
> *They leave their rooms bereft and bare*
> *And we can't find them anywhere.*
> *Please, please, when you vacate your chairs*
> *Leave your buildings by the stairs*
> *Let us know when you go;*
> *Pick up the phone and Dial 'O'.*

From Diamond Sculls to Golden Handcuffs

In the newly merged partnership, those who came from RHB had few illusions that, despite fine talk about unions, they had been taken over. But they did not mind: the market began to recover in 1975 and, despite fears about hyperinflation, everyone got back into the habit of making money. RHB's proven expertise in property and insurance soon proved its worth, adding depth and credibility to Rowe & Pitman's all-encompassing and therefore sometimes disparate research efforts. Meanwhile Rowe & Pitman made headway in its proven fields of corporate finance, gilts and, increasingly, fund management.

An important part of the rationale for the merger had been the lack of business overlap. If any tensions now surfaced, they were between Corporate Finance (a Rowe & Pitman stronghold) and the improved Research Department, an RHB redoubt which jealously guarded its independence. In 1976, three months before Rowe & Pitman was due to bring the insurance broker Willis Faber to the market, the research team issued a circular rating the firm a sell. The corporate financiers were not amused. Nor was Willis Faber, which demoted Rowe & Pitman as its lead broker.

Life was not always easy for the newly merged partnership. A May 1975 memo suggests that chaos was regularly just around the corner:

> Bargains have recently averaged 400 per day and, although we should be able to process this volume, the settlement departments have been strained: contracts go out late, the computer has indigestion, partners are signing until 10 p.m. The contract dept. staff is particularly fatigued. But the reduction of branch bank business should help. We had a credit balance of over £200,000 overnight money on 7th May, but expect to have to borrow heavily again for the 13th May account day for which total sales are £34m, and the purchases £31m. If the electricity supply industry were forced to make power cuts, operation of the computer might be difficult to guarantee, but we could turn to Datasolve who have a private generator.

The computer was a new ICL 9000 mainframe, introduced under the aegis of Guy Kingsbury, the Information Technology

Manager, and later updated to an ICL 2900. Luckily RHB brought two experienced office administrators in Gordon English and Norman Andrews, who soon took control of the overstretched settlements operation. The capable English subsequently became Office Manager and Financial Controller.

The longer-term problems remained, however. Assuming Mackworth-Young's mantle as partnership soothsayer, Nick Verey, a young high-flyer in the Corporate Finance Department could see that the London market was moving in the direction of New York, where vast investment banks were now the norm, providing a one-stop service by combining the functions of making markets, selling shares and running investment funds. In London, the future for separate jobbers and brokers even seemed uncertain. But Rowe & Pitman remained strangely unequipped for the new financial environment. As Verey pointed out in June 1975, three areas – execution, research and corporate finance – were becoming particularly important on Wall Street, following the introduction of negotiated commissions there. But Rowe & Pitman had no active full-time partner in charge of two of these areas, and few candidates who might reasonably assume such positions.

Rowe & Pitman's prospects were not improved when the bull market ended the following year and the City, and its whole *raison d'être*, came under fire from the incumbent Labour government. The way forward seemed to be through further expansion. Already in late 1976 the question of introducing outside capital into the partnership had been raised. The names of possible suitors, such as County Bank, were bandied about, and the prospect of Rowe & Pitman's own stock market flotation was raised. At the time County Bank was Rowe & Pitman's largest client, entirely as a result of its turnover in gilts. After County, the next twelve clients were the Kuwait Investment Office, Hambros Bank, Ennia Insurance, Morgan Grenfell, S.G. Warburg, Robeco, Robert Fleming, J. Henry Schroder Wagg, Barclays Group, Prudential Assurance, Fidelity Management and Research, and Rowan Merlin. The KIO account had been boosted following the merger, for RHB's links with the Kuwaitis

– for whom it had acted in the takeover of St Martin's – were stronger than Rowe & Pitman's, and this proved an important asset in the brave new world of petrodollar power. The respected KIO consolidated its ties with the merged firm, providing much business in the late 1970s and early 1980s, particularly to Rowe & Pitman's new overseas arms in North America and the Far East.

In January 1977, Nigel Elwes advocated that the merged firm should actively look for outside capital. He painted a familiar picture:

> We need more capital in the firm to give us a bigger base from which to expand our sales and improve our profitability so that when the decision is finally taken to obtain a quotation we are big and profitable enough to secure a successful launching. It should also be remembered that our present excess over the minimum margin of solvency is not enormous and could become dangerously small if we had another sustained period of low activity.
>
> The position is likely to be aggravated in the fairly near future as partners who control a large percentage of the total retire and not only withdraw equity but also substantial amounts of 'B' capital and 'D' accounts which we are unlikely to be able to replenish from within the business. In addition, the Bank of England may require us substantially to increase our capital in the fairly near future if we wish to continue the present level of activity (let alone increase the business) in money broking.

By no means all the partners were convinced that this was the best way forward. Corney, in particular, was happy to take his retirement in 1977, before any further dilution of the firm's basic identity occurred. Sir Peter Vanneck opted out for a different reason. The nephew of Andrew Vanneck, he had been toiling without much pay at Phillips & Drew when his friend Everard Hambro recommended him to Julian Martin Smith in 1961. At Rowe & Pitman, he made the rounds of Rothschilds and Kleinwort Benson, while, as a corporate broker, he took over his uncle's Shell connection and visited a variety of companies, including Pilkington's, in the North-West, where he had served during the war. In 1968 he agreed to take over from Peter Henderson as Rowe & Pitman's voice on the Stock Exchange Council. This led him to accept a profusion of institutional and honorific posts in the City, becoming Deputy Chairman of the Council from 1973 to 1975 and Lord Mayor of London in 1977/8. The following year, he decided to abandon stockbroking and take up politics as Conservative Member of the European Parliament for Cleveland.

As an accountant, even the enthusiastic Elwes could recognize that fiscal problems might arise if a big outside investor took equity in an unincorporated partnership such as Rowe & Pitman. An alternative possibility was that the firm could offer stakes in specific areas, such as money broking, foreign business or fund management. The last of these was beginning to feature more prominently in the firm's corporate profile. Two forces in particular were working to achieve this. One was the tremendous growth in all sorts of funds, many operating across borders (not all needing direct management; some simply wanted to use Rowe & Pitman to buy large blocks of shares). The other was a realization that Rowe & Pitman could benefit from playing this game itself, perhaps even running its own funds.

At the start of the 1970s, fund management was loosely found in two areas of Rowe & Pitman's general business – the pension service (which was linked to Research and part of the Operations Room) and the Private Client Department. Prodded by the two Jameses, Ogilvy and D'Albiac, these two strands started to coalesce. One step in this direction was the setting up of two unit trusts, the Rowan International and Rowan Securities Funds, in 1972 and 1973 respectively (though these were initially reserved for private clients).

For the time being, however, investment management failed to take off. Some people argue that it continued to be held back by inefficient administration and, in particular, that bugbear of the time, a slow settlements procedure. Others say it was simply not very good at developing and marketing investment ideas. Despite reduced revenue (down from £1 million in 1972 to £574,000 in

1974), costs remained virtually static, and in 1973 and 1974 this side of the business dipped into the red. (At the time Rowe & Pitman was responsible for 5,833 managed clients, 2,062 of them with portfolios worth less than £10,000.) Given the depressed economic circumstances in the firm in general, fund management was seen as a luxury, if not a millstone.

Further hands-on experience showed that a serious conflict of interest could arise between Rowe & Pitman's different roles as corporate financier, stockbroker and fund manager. As a London director of the US Trust, managed by his friend, Bob Buist, Ogilvy knew that American financial institutions had already coped with this problem. Inspired by Buist, he went to New York to observe how the investment bank Donaldson Lufkin Jenrette had managed to keep its institutional investment arm, Alliance Capital, separate from its private client business, Wood Stuthers (in later City parlance, by establishing a Chinese wall). He became convinced that Rowe & Pitman needed to set up an autonomous investment management company, with its own offices and executives. He also felt that, as evidence of its independence, and despite counter-arguments that this might seem to encroach on the preserve of merchant banks, this new section should anticipate its competitors and begin to charge fees to its clients. The development of a two-centre business (in the Stock Exchange Tower and in City Gate House) in 1975 seemed to favour such an initiative, as did the link with RHB, which operated two successful unit trusts, Merlin and Merlin High Yield, and which had already managed a handful of discretionary funds for local-government clients.

In June 1975, shortly after the merger, Ogilvy floated a proposal that Rowe & Pitman should establish a fund management company along these lines as part of a joint venture with US Trust. In a period of high turnover, he argued, 'more of the company's business could be executed by other stockbrokers, whilst in a period of low turnover Rowe & Pitman's revenue could be correspondingly boosted'. All in all, this solution was touted as one that would help make fund management profitable.

But other partners feared that Rowe & Pitman would be

dwarfed by US Trust. Eventually in 1976 it was decided to press ahead with a wholly owned company, known as Rowan Investment Management Services. As a compromise Bob Buist was hired from US Trust – initially as a 'consultant', later as a director – with responsibility for the new unit's American investments. From the start Rowan embarked on a process of weeding out its smaller, less profitable clients. Bank branches were among the first accounts to go.

Even then Rowan's problems were not over because there were two different approaches to fund management. D'Albiac wanted to stay in the Stock Exchange and service his clients (institutional and others) as an old-fashioned broker with direct access to the floor of the House. Ogilvy, on the other hand, was convinced that Rowan should emphasize its independence from Rowe & Pitman (and physical separation was at least one way of doing this). His underlying point was that, in order to charge fees, Rowan needed to buy in investment research from all comers, including rival brokers, and also sometimes, as a quid pro quo, to channel its purchases through these same competitors. The differing perspectives of the market entertained by City Gate House and the 'Tower Unit' probably held back fund management's growth. But at least Rowan was a recognizable entity which added value to Rowe & Pitman, and could, if required one day, be put up for sale.

However the jewel in the Rowe & Pitman crown was increasingly its integrated corporate broking and equity sales operation, where Peter Wilmot-Sitwell was managing to weld his 'can-do' Operations Room experience onto Mackworth-Young's City know-how to produce a team that was as deft at wooing corporate clients as merchant banks, and as professional over pricing an issue as distributing it in the market-place.

On the sixteenth floor of the Stock Exchange Tower, Wilmot-Sitwell sat in the middle of a bustling open-plan office, which theoretically allowed easy access between an enhanced Research Department, a variety of dedicated teams selling to the institutions, and Stuart Stradling's core of corporate brokers who liaised directly with businesses on new-issue work.

From Diamond Sculls to Golden Handcuffs

The working day would now start at 8.30 with an analyst presenting his latest nuggets of research. (Dissemination of this information was not always easy, as the loudspeaker system had a habit of breaking down.) Reporting to Wilmot-Sitwell, Nick Verey then co-ordinated the sales teams, each with its own field of specialization – gilts, fixed interest, insurance, property, UK equities, mining and overseas. The set-up was reasonably fluid: for example, Peter Hardy, the property specialist, liked to do his own research and selling. When a salesman received an order, he would phone down to the 'box' (presided over by the Market Partner Peter Heming Johnson). If a specialist dealer was not available, a blue button would seek him out on the floor of the House.

The system was evolving all the time. As late as December 1982, Verey complained that when the firm was not doing 'special deals' or enjoying 'big equity days', its market share regularly fell below 3 per cent. One reason, he felt, was that out of thirty-six partners, only three – George Pilkington, Peter Thompson and Henry Pelham – were 'big hitters' dedicated to UK equity selling. There were too many partners flitting around with no particular sales responsibilities.

Nevertheless, corporate broking had seen a steady build-up of business following the slump of 1974. Wilmot-Sitwell recalled that the market's nadir came with Burmah Oil's failure on New Year's Eve 1974. The following day, a Saturday, he was shooting at Sandringham, where that old friend of Rowe & Pitman, the Queen Mother, asked him how the firm was coping. He kept his real thoughts to himself, only allowing himself to tell Her Majesty that the situation was 'worrying'. On the Sunday, the royal party went to church, along with Wilmot-Sitwell and his wife, who happened to be celebrating their fifteenth wedding anniversary. Afterwards the Queen Mother announced that she had prayed that the market would improve. The very next morning, Harold Lever, a Treasury minister, made the first encouraging noises about the economy to emerge from the Government for a long time. Thereafter the gloom began to lift, and when Wilmot-Sitwell next saw the Queen Mother, he pleased her by saying that he thought she must have a direct line to God.

For the first year after that the market was dominated by rights issues. Rowe & Pitman played its part, raising money this way for Prudential Assurance, United Biscuits, Siebens Oil and Gas, Legal and General, Land Securities Investment Trust, Plessey and, finally, ICI, for whom £203 million was successfully raised in May 1976. The next few months were quieter, as insurance and property shares, an old RHB speciality, fell out of favour. But the good times returned the following summer. In July 1977 Rowe & Pitman arranged a modest £18.8 million rights issue for British Sugar Corporation (BSC), which is memorable largely as an example of the firm's growing authority. Corporate clients now came less from school, family or grouse-moor connections, and more from winning the confidence of hard-headed industry bosses. BSC's Chairman John Beckett was to feature in several of Rowe & Pitman's placings in the following decade.

More spectacular was Rowe & Pitman's involvement in June that year, as one of the brokers in the first big privatization exercise, a £564 million offer for sale of a quarter of the government's stake in British Petroleum (BP). Rowe & Pitman's role in this flotation confirmed its status as a big player in the emerging equity markets.

Times were certainly changing, as Elwes's experience shows. Although he was principally taken up with partnership affairs, he also had more general Operations Room duties. On the one hand, he was Corporate Partner in charge of the firm's relationship with Shell (which required considerable work on taxation questions without much feedback in the form of new profitable issues). On the other, he was an equities salesman with a client list including Touche Remnant, Robert Fleming, Murray Johnstone, Legal and General and London Trust, the Old Pilkington connection for which he had complete discretion. (The established Rowe & Pitman networks still operated strongly, if a little less overtly. The River Plate and General, the other investment trust whose business came to Rowe & Pitman via Malcolm Pilkington was chaired by Julian Martin Smith who, on his retirement from Rowe & Pitman in April 1979, had taken over from Malcolm's nephew – and Charlie's son – Alec Pilkington. Alec's own son, George Pilkington, had joined Rowe & Pitman from Eton in 1968, becoming a partner eleven years later, and was now himself a top salesman in the Operations Room. To complete the picture, Elwes was Martin Smith's nephew – a relationship that office wags would mock good-naturedly in calling the firm Smith and Nephew.)

As the BP sale drew near, Elwes, a racing enthusiast, was looking forward to Royal Ascot. In the old days, he would have taken the day off, but Wilmot-Sitwell, in the Operations Room, told him he could not go until he had placed a certain amount of stock. Elwes was forced to come to the office in half-change. After consulting his list of contacts, he telephoned Touche Remnant and pleaded, 'You've got to help me.' He only missed the first race that day.

The BP offer helped cement Rowe & Pitman's shaky ties with Warburg. After the débâcle of British Aluminium in 1959, the two firms had remained at arms' length for much of the following decade, until Mackworth-Young shared a Laporte issue with Warburg's chairman David Scholey in 1969. Three years later, a Rowe & Pitman client, Sainsbury's, insisted on using Warburg for an offer for sale which created some Stock Exchange history. At the time the supermarket group was capitalized at £117 million, but it only wanted to raise £14.5 million, which was below the 25 per cent statutory minimum that City regulations required the company to put up for sale. So Rowe & Pitman successfully petitioned the Stock Exchange for a reduction in this threshold. At the same time it created another precedent by ensuring that members of the Sainsbury's board were not required to provide their home addresses on the issue documents. (It helped, of course, that Wilmot-Sitwell, Mackworth-Young and Milne were all personal friends of the Sainsbury family.)

But while stockbroker and merchant bank worked well enough over Sainsbury's, their relationship came embarrassingly unstuck after Rowe & Pitman had targeted Warburg as an important source of business in the period following Mackworth-Young's departure. However this coincided with the 1974 stock-market slump, and the first issue that came Rowe & Pitman's way from Warburg was a debenture for the St Regis Paper Company that Wilmot-Sitwell has no qualms in admitting, 'we cocked up'. Rowe & Pitman thought it could place the issue, and failed. 'At the time we were like chalk and cheese,' recalled Wilmot-Sitwell. 'They were a tough Jewish bank, and we were Hooray Henries enjoying ourselves.'

Five years later things had altered, and one easily overlooked reason for the transformation was the cool head which ran the organization. When Julian Martin Smith came to retire in April 1979, William Robson wrote to him, 'You took us through a very unpleasant time of depression in the early seventies when many of us were nearly dead financially. You went on to lay the foundations of the firm we now are and I am sure that much of its strength lies in our having built up a strong overseas business.'

One secret was the atmosphere at the quarterly partners' meetings where, Robson observed:

> We all sat listening respectfully. Under your benign chairmanship Bill [Mackworth-Young] usually outlined any new proposition you both had in mind. This was greeted with silence if it was a 'goer' and with mumbles if it wasn't. Anyway, at about six o'clock, you usually went over to the sideboard and got a dark brown or, if you didn't, we did. Then you knew and we soon came to know that it was no good talking about anything serious after that because we would all become argumentative or even scratchy. So we all had a drink and went home, and the item which had been 'controversial' would be sorted out quietly before the next meeting. And the decisions were almost always right.

If that sounds sentimental, it only reflected what was thought in the market.

9 Into the Nineties

A LADDISH JAK cartoon can be found in the downstairs lavatories of a couple of partners' houses. It shows a stockbroker type gingerly donning his clothes, while a woman in *déshabillé*, who is clearly his mistress, looks on admiringly. 'The City's understanding of a Dawn Raid!', runs the caption.

Lancy Hugh Smith would have approved of neither the cartoon nor the event that occasioned it. For in 1980 Rowe & Pitman made it onto the front pages. It did so by spectacularly entering the market on the morning of Tuesday 12 February 1980 to purchase 15 per cent of the stock of the British-owned mining finance house Consolidated Goldfields on behalf of its long-time client, the Anglo American Corporation of South Africa. And it did so with such bravado that a new Conservative government, committed as it was to free enterprise, was forced to mount an investigation to see if its takeover rules had been flouted.

There had been a couple of dry runs for this operation. Back in 1977 Peter Wilmot-Sitwell had put his back out and was resting at home, reading *Crash of 79*, the then credible scare story of how Arab 'petro-sheikhs' manipulated the price of oil to put the stock market in free-fall and take over the commanding heights of American industry. He had just reached the last page when he had a call from Julian Martin Smith, who needed to see him on urgent business. Making light of his pain, he travelled into the office and then, as his Senior Partner directed, on to Morgan Grenfell. There his old friend Bill Mackworth-Young, by now Deputy Chairman and Chief Executive of the merchant bank,

Into the Nineties

told him in strictest confidence that the Shah of Iran wanted to buy 10 per cent of Arnold Weinstock's General Electric Company (GEC). But before committing himself, the Shah required a cast-iron guarantee that he would be successful.

Wilmot-Sitwell knew GEC well, having master-minded its 1967 acquisition of AEI. What is more, Mackworth-Young had worked with Wilmot-Sitwell on that takeover, and their two firms had subsequently liaised in Iran, where Morgan Grenfell had a representative office. After discussion, they hatched a scheme whereby, instead of underwriting, they would in effect overwrite by approaching large holders of GEC stock and saying: 'We want to buy a stake in GEC, and we are prepared to pay substantially above the market price. However, if we fail to obtain the requisite number of shares, will you – in return for a prearranged fee, which you will be paid, whatever happens – guarantee to provide any extra shares we may need?' That way Morgan and Rowe & Pitman could not fail, for either they bought their shares in the market in the usual way, or else they acquired them directly from these institutional owners.

In the event the deal was scuppered, partly because Wilmot-Sitwell thought it essential to have GEC's approval, and the non-executive directors were wary about proceeding, and partly because Ayatollah Khomeini put paid to the Shah's grandiose schemes.

Two years later, shortly after Alan Hurst-Brown had taken over as Senior Partner, Wilmot-Sitwell was summoned to a different bank, Hambros, which had an American client, the Continental Corporation, wanting to buy into Stenhouse, the British insurance-broking group. Asked his opinion how this could be achieved, Wilmot-Sitwell, with his Iranian experience fresh in his mind, suggested that Continental should offer to pay over the odds for a set number of shares for a specific period of time, after which the offer would close. Rowe & Pitman placed an announcement in the evening papers on Friday, 17 August 1979, stating that, at the start of business on Monday, it intended to buy Stenhouse shares on behalf of Continental. The British company's shares were suspended at 87 pence. On the Monday morning, Rowe & Pitman and its jobbers were inundated with sellers. They bought 5 million shares at 110 pence (including one million from Save and Prosper which liquidated two-thirds of its Stenhouse holdings), another 1 million at 100 pence, and the remaining 1.59 million at 97.5 pence.

Brickbats were quickly hurled in Rowe & Pitman's direction. The firm was accused of acting against the spirit of Stock Exchange regulations by offering a preferential price to a small group of customers. Wilmot-Sitwell defended himself, 'Lloyd's rules specified that an overseas broker could only acquire a maximum 20 per cent of a Lloyd's broker like Stenhouse, so holders knew that once we got that amount that would be the end. As we were paying over the odds they had an incentive to accept.' Nevertheless the concept of the 'dawn raid' had been born (though within Rowe & Pitman it continued to be known as the 'Stenhouse method').

Stenhouse was only the dress rehearsal for a much more daring show. During August 1979 Oliver Baring, the partner in charge of mining finance, began to notice increased activity in the shares of Consolidated Goldfields, a British conglomerate which owned 49 per cent of the highly profitable Gold Fields of South Africa. Surmising that a predator was building up a stake, Baring found that two companies, General Mining and the Rembrandt Group, were indeed stalking 'Consgold' and, as he knew through regular discussions with Johannesburg, Anglo American would not be happy with the consequent change in the balance of power in the local Chamber of Mines.

Alerted by Baring, Anglo decided, as a stalling exercise if nothing else, to build up a position in Consgold itself. But it was determined to keep its interest quiet. One means was to use financial rand rather than sterling: if its orders came to Rowe & Pitman via Anglo's Johannesburg broker, Davis Borkum & Hare, this would cover any dealings with an additional cloak of anonymity. In addition, a company acquiring 5 per cent of another had, according to the Stock Exchange code, to disclose it. But Anglo's widespread corporate structure offered it a controversial way round this bureaucratic detail. It opted to buy its Consgold shares through a variety of seemingly unrelated offshoots.

On 26 October Rowe & Pitman duly told the jobbers, Akroyd & Smithers that it had a large order for Consgold, and to start accumulating stock. Quietly over the course of the autumn Rowe & Pitman built up Anglo's holding through 5 per cent and up to 10 per cent. It was further helped by the fact that, under existing regulations, it did not have to register the transactions, because dealing in the stock of Consgold and other companies with dual London and Johannesburg registrations had not yet been included in the new computerized Talisman process, which automatically registered shares without waiting for settlement.

It was not until the New Year that Consgold started to worry about the amount of stock going off the register. Realizing it did not know who was buying, it asked the Stock Exchange for an inquiry. By now Rowe & Pitman was pressing Anglo to use the 'Stenhouse method' to increase its stake to around 25 per cent (just below the 29 per cent threshold at which a formal bid had to be launched). This would mean buying 16.5 million shares in one fell swoop, but its client was not convinced that this could be achieved. It was only when Consgold chairman Lord Errol 'upped the ante' by asking the Department of Trade (where he himself had been the Minister) for an inquiry that Anglo began to contemplate taking Rowe & Pitman's advice. Then things moved very quickly.

On the afternoon of Monday, 11 February, Wilmot-Sitwell telephoned Julian Ogilvie Thompson, the Anglo Chief Executive, in Johannesburg. He recalled that Ogilvie Thompson 'asked me, for the first time, at what price we could acquire enough shares to bring the holding up to 25 per cent. The asset value of the company was £6.50 a share, and I thought we could acquire the balance at about £6.00 – the price in the morning having been £5.35'.

Still Ogilvie Thompson thought it unlikely that he would want to act the following day, when he was scheduled to attend an important meeting in Cape Town. But overnight Anglo

Chairman Harry Oppenheimer came in on the act. At 7.15 on the Tuesday morning a restless Wilmot-Sitwell received a call at his London flat asking him to get in touch with Neil Clarke, the Anglo Finance Director. 'I rang Neil in his office and he said that they had now decided to do a raid. We agreed between us, for reasons that now seem somewhat opaque, that the best price would be £6.15. As they already had 21 million shares, our order was to buy a further 16.5 million. We then took all the necessary steps as far as our market's rules and regulations were concerned and carried out the raid.'

Journalist Bill Jamieson recorded what happened next in his book *Goldstrike!*

> The price was marked up on the 'pitch' and fed to the computer screen market price display system. Within Rowe & Pitman itself, near bedlam had broken out: 30 staff were briefed and ordered to hit the phones to buy stocks from 200 clients. There was no time to go through the share register and select holders of large blocks; each member of staff went through his own client list asking them if they held Gold Fields shares and telling them of the bid. By 9.50 a.m., Rowe & Pitman had received more offers of stock from clients than were needed and scaling down was necessary. By 9.55 a.m. the operation was complete.

Rowe & Pitman subsequently had to attend inquiries by the Department of Trade and the Stock Exchange's Takeover Panel. There was even a debate in the House of Commons which led to changes in the Companies Act governing large-scale share purchases. Julian Martin Smith, who had joined the Board of Rowe & Pitman (South Africa), saw fit to write to the Prime Minister, Margaret Thatcher, drawing her attention to the threat to free enterprise posed by potential government regulation. The firm's notoriety was ensured when Lord Shawcross, Chairman of the Takeover Panel, launched a swingeing attack on the 'dawn raid' (as the Stenhouse method was now universally known). By offering one price for the rich institutional investor and another (much less) for the proverbial maiden aunt, this technique rode roughshod over the principle that all shareholders should be treated equally, he argued.

'We are not doing anything unfair,' countered Alan Hurst-Brown. 'We are dealing in the market place, and shareholders should be prepared to accept the rigours of the market. Aunty Fanny would not lose out if she did the sensible thing and gave her stockbroker discretion, and anyway, most of the shares we are dealing with belong to institutions, which in turn belong to small investors.'

Within Rowe & Pitman the circumstances surrounding the raid – its audacity, its precision and its success – were matters of considerable pride. On 19 March, the Board of Management took the unusual step of minuting its congratulations, and adding:

> Particular mention must be made to OAGB [Oliver Baring] who was the prime initiator of the business. It is normally considered invidious to make special mention of a particular piece of business, but not only was the whole operation one of enormous proportions but the clinching deal carried out on Tuesday 12th February is believed to be the largest ever carried out by a single firm of stockbrokers.

Dawn raids were now headline news, and Rowe & Pitman, its leading practitioner, reaped the kudos. Over the next few months it executed several similar coups, hoovering up great chunks of companies like Revertex and Carpets International in carefully orchestrated share-buying forays. One of its most audacious operations was conducted on behalf of Charter Consolidated, another building block in the Anglo American empire, which, in May 1980, acquired 28.4% of the mining equipment company, Anderson Strathclyde – all within twenty minutes, and at nearly a quarter above the market price. 'Rowe & Pitman have done it again,' commented Lex in the *Financial Times*.

Rowe & Pitman was on a roll. One of its established clients, an RHB connection, was Godfrey Bradman, boss of the publicly quoted property company Rosehaugh. In 1981 Bradman conceived a plan to detach the British arm of Woolworth from its American parent but, despite Rowe & Pitman's success in raising £130 million from institutions and interested parties including GEC chairman Arnold Weinstock, he was rebuffed.

In April the following year, Wilmot-Sitwell succeeded Hurst-Brown as Rowe & Pitman's Senior Partner. (At one stage it had appeared that he might share the job with David Innes, but the latter preferred to remain behind the scenes in the invaluable role of Finance Partner.) Wilmot-Sitwell had only been in charge one day when he was approached by Peter Hardy, the old RHB hand who overlooked property clients, who told him in strictest confidence that Bradman was once more looking to acquire British Woolworth. Only this time the running was being made by Charterhouse, a merchant bank with which Rowe & Pitman had good relations, because the American parent needed reassuring that the deal was not simply property speculation. Victor Blank, Charterhouse's corporate finance chief, formed a new company, Paternoster Stores (later Kingfisher), with John Beckett, Rowe & Pitman's old friend from British Sugar (recently swallowed by Berisford) as Chairman and the capable Alan Hurst-Brown as one of the directors. Rowe & Pitman's job was to help raise the £165 million (roughly half the overall cost) needed from institutions to finance the deal. Rowe & Pitman trawled through its contacts book and got the Prudential, the Kuwait Investment Office and several pension funds on board.

Rowe & Pitman's reputation for innovation was not confined to corporate finance. In the gilts sector, it had in 1981 pioneered quoted yearling bonds for building societies – in this case, the Nationwide. With a new bond every month, yielding a generous ⅛ per cent commission, this skilful but not wildly exciting series of issues earned the firm an estimated £250,000 over the next eight years – a useful contribution to anyone's bottom line. It was supplemented in 1986 by three long-dated index-linked bonds for the Nationwide, the first ever non-government index-linked bonds.

Inevitably, in the heady atmosphere of the times, such instruments were eagerly sought for their portfolios by both corporate and county council treasurers. Rowe & Pitman's gilts expertise helped raise its profile in previously untapped sectors of public finance, leading directly to the acquisition of new county council accounts by the firm's fund management side – a fine example of the different arms of the partnership working for each other.

Rowe & Pitman's success was supported by a growing Research Department, where traditional sector-orientated reports were now supplemented by a much wider range of macro-economic analysis. John Shephard arrived from Mullens to develop the firm's monthly gilt-edged bulletin into a weekly publication that was underpinned by a much-sought-after digest of key statistics. Ian Harwood's valuable overall economic research was backed up by outside consultants, notably Walter Eltis, a fellow of Exeter College, Oxford (later to become head of the National Economic Development Council), who wrote a quarterly economic bulletin which helped stimulate thinking on topics such as future interest rates and inflation. Eltis came to Rowe & Pitman through Laurie Baraghanath, a maverick academic turned stockbroker, who had himself been recruited to RHB just before the merger by Derek Childs. Baraghanath had excellent connections in the Australian mining industry, where his early advocacy of the uranium mine Pan-Continental made him a personal fortune. Once a don at St Catherine's College, Oxford, he brought to Rowe & Pitman his prize pupil, Paddy Fitzpatrick, later one of the firm's most effective equity salesmen.

Rowe & Pitman's corporate clients could now count on an integrated approach, linking research, sales and professional advice, and all overseen by a competent partner. In the competitive 1980s, some businessmen needed convincing of the firm's merits. Nick Verey, for example, worked hard to convince Alec Monk of the Dee Corporation that he needed the services of a broker. Monk argued that he and his associates could handle the expensive paperwork accompanying an issue very well themselves. Wooed by Robin Newman, Sir Patrick Meaney, boss of Thomas Tilling, was more sympathetic. His firm 'spewed out equity' (as another partner delicately put it) until it was bought by BTR in a hotly contested £600 million takeover in the spring of 1983. In his next job as Chairman of the Rank Organisation, Meaney showed his appreciation by appointing Rowe & Pitman as the company's broker.

By this time the City was becoming frenetic and highly politicized as a reforming Conservative administration under Margaret Thatcher sought to speed the ongoing deregulation of the Stock Exchange, leading to 'Big Bang' in 1986. Further privatization of state industries was high on the agenda but, as earnest of the openness it wanted in the financial services industry, the Government was determined to show that it acted without fear or favour in appointing its advisers. Thus when the Department of Energy came to privatize Britoil in November 1982, its merchant bank, Warburg, held a 'beauty contest' of stockbrokers to find the most appropriate for the deal. Determined to be in on this lucrative act, Rowe & Pitman pulled out the stops to win the mandate, and was successful. In the spirit of the times, the issue was put out to tender but, on this occasion, failed to inspire much interest from investors. If this was something of a set-back, Rowe & Pitman was unconcerned. The Britoil sale only improved its now solid working relationship with Warburg.

Rowe & Pitman proved particularly adept in 'special situations', as was shown by its nimble footwork when two rival consortia tried to wrest control of its client, the troubled British helicopter manufacturer Westland, in a divisive battle in late 1985. On the one side was ranged Sikorsky, a subsidiary of the giant US-based United Technologies; on the other a powerful European group, which included British Aerospace and GEC. The virtues of an American versus a European 'solution' split the Cabinet, leading to the resignation of the Secretaries of State for Defence, Michael Heseltine (an enthusiastic pro-European), and for Industry, Leon Brittan. It also created a notably topsy-turvy environment for Rowe & Pitman to work in. As Westland's Chairman, Sir John Cuckney, tilted towards Sikorsky, Wilmot-Sitwell and his team also began acting for the American firm. On one occasion Sikorsky bought more stock than it was allowed under complicated rules pertaining at the time, and Rowe & Pitman had to offload it quickly. Then, as Sikorsky sensed

Into the Nineties

victory, a series of mystery buyers of large tranches of Westland stock started appearing. As Westland's price rose, Wilmot-Sitwell was in the thick of it, trying to coax the company's shares out of institutions such as the Prudential, which could no longer afford to look a gift horse in the mouth. The exact role of these buyers, and their relationship to one another, was later the subject of an inconclusive parliamentary inquiry. Eventually, Sikorsky gained control, with the Rowe & Pitman Senior Partner enjoying a unique perspective, since the weekend before the deal was clinched the new Secretary of State for Trade and Industry, Paul Channon, was staying with him at his house in Hampshire.

If, in these feverish times, Westland showed the Stock Exchange being pushed to the limits, the Guinness affair less than a year later saw it topple over the edge. On this occasion Rowe & Pitman (perhaps thankfully in retrospect) acted for Argyll, the loser in a bitter City battle to gain control of the whisky group, Distillers. The winner was Guinness, but its resort to illegal concert parties to ramp up the price of its shares resulted in its Chairman, Ernest Saunders, going to prison.

By then the long-mooted 'Big Bang' had actually taken place and Rowe & Pitman's corporate status had changed out of all recognition. In keeping with the spirit of the times, it had merged in April 1986 with Mercury Securities, the holding company for S.G. Warburg, Rowe & Pitman's closest merchant bank ally over the previous hectic few years. The partnership begun in Threadneedle Street in late 1894 had lasted not quite a hundred years.

Its apotheosis happened quickly as outside and inside forces came together. On the external front, the rapid take-up of new technology in the 1970s made British financial markets seem slow, small and insular. Capital-raising was now a global business, and the Stock Exchange's quaint division of its market into 'single capacity' brokers and jobbers no longer sufficed. As Nick Verey had noted, the American model was now the norm, and that meant large-scale investment banks, or one-stop boutiques for all financial services from raising capital through market-making to fund management.

On an institutional level, London still took some time to recognize that a large-scale transformation of the City was in the offing. The Stock Exchange acknowledged the trend, as far as stockbroking was concerned, when in June 1982 it agreed to allow outside businesses to take up to 29.9 per cent stake in its member firms. But it was loath to contemplate more basic reform, remaining obstinate in the face of often inept legislative attempts to force it to change its ways of operating. Only in July 1983 was a deal struck whereby the Government dropped restrictive practices proceedings against the Stock Exchange in return for the latter embarking on an active policy of deregulation, including the abandonment of both fixed minimum commissions and the distinction between brokers and jobbers. The Exchange set a date in October 1986, dubbed 'Big Bang', for the introduction of these reforms.

This whole process provided the impetus for Elwes, a long-time advocate of the need for extra capital, to redouble his efforts to secure an outside partner for Rowe & Pitman. Working closely with David Innes as head of what was codenamed Project 84 or even simply Godmother, he enlisted the specialist help of Thomson McLintock to put a value on the partnership. In early 1982 the figures showed that, based on assets of £5 million and a profit the previous year of £3.17 million, the firm, with its subsidiaries, could be capitalized at around £13 million (taking a multiple of ten times this profit, net of 52 per cent tax). On Elwes's initial premise of selling 20 per cent of the firm, this would mean a capital injection of £3.75 million, with £1.4 million going straight to the partners for goodwill (subject to capital gains tax).

Then the difficult process of finding a suitable partner began. Even at this stage, Morgan Grenfell seemed an obvious candidate: the two firms had an unwritten agreement that, in such circumstances, they would join up. But during the 1980s Morgan Grenfell was aggressively developing its corporate finance side (in a manner which was to culminate in the Guinness affair) and claimed to have no interest in a mere stockbroker. In any case, Rowe & Pitman soon learned to steer clear of obvious merchant bank suitors like Morgan Grenfell or even Hambros, because to have one on board would inevitably drive away business from the other.

During 1983 Elwes and Wilmot-Sitwell saw around thirty prospective stakeholders, including Merrill Lynch and the Bank of North Carolina. Finally, in December 1983, the right fit was found much closer to home in Charter Consolidated, the mining finance house – British-domiciled but very much part of the Oppenheimer diamond and gold empire – which brought together Cecil Rhodes's British South Africa Company (the Chartered Company) with Central Mining, the old 'Corner House' which, under the aegis of Julius Wernher and Alfred Beit, had been so influential in the 'Kaffir' boom of the 1890s. In one way or another, Rowe & Pitman had acted as brokers to the company for over half a century. Indeed Esmond Baring was working on Charter Consolidated's incorporation at the time of his death in 1963.

Not only did this link bring Rowe & Pitman cosily within the broad Anglo American empire for which it had worked so long, but also Charter seemed an ideal match. With Neil Clarke as its Chief Executive (Anglo's Finance Director at the time of the Consgold dawn raid), Charter had a long purse and, although active in financial services in the United States through Minorco's holding in Salomon Brothers, had no obvious ambitions to control Rowe & Pitman.

In the event Rowe & Pitman did very much better than Elwes had predicted only two years earlier. Gross commissions had doubled, it is true, in the intervening period, but Charter had to stump up £16.2 million to buy a 29.9 per cent stake on 9 January 1984. That very same day Rowe & Pitman also announced that it had set up a joint venture with Akroyd & Smithers, now its closest jobbers, to market and deal in international equities in New York. The details of this latter venture, which required Akroyd to contribute £11 million and Rowe & Pitman £6 million, were finalized in an all-night session in the Savoy Hotel, where Rowe & Pitman was represented by David Brooke, David Russell and Nigel Elwes. In the new joint venture, known as ROWAK, both firms looked forward to the Stock Exchange's relaxation of the principle of 'single capacity' two years later. But for the time being British brokers and jobbers could only work together in overseas markets.

In one way this New York link underlined the resilience of Rowe & Pitman's foreign businesses. The original Rowe & Pitman Inc. based in San Francisco had prospered mightily. In 1981 it spawned a new East Coast office in Boston. By 1984, it was contributing £4.7 million (or nearly a fifth) to Rowe & Pitman's world-wide revenues of £25 million. The local brokers, headed by Norman Weller, were rewarded by being given a gradually larger share of the US business (up to 10.8 per cent by 1986). However, by headquartering its operations in New York, ROWAK no longer enjoyed Rowe & Pitman Inc.'s niche roles in San Francisco and Boston while, at the same time, opening itself up to the full force of international competition. David Russell wistfully recalls the number of top salesmen – among them, Gordon Begg, Nigel Pilkington (a cousin of George), David Ruck-Keene and Nick Banister, later head of the London operations of ABN Amro – who passed through ROWAK before succumbing to the advances of rival companies with larger purses.

Rowe & Pitman's Far East operation (centred on Hong Kong and Japan) also turned in healthy profits (£2.41 million in 1984). This picture was only marred in May 1985, when Douglas Ho, the local executive who held the Rowe & Pitman seat on Hong Kong's Kan Ngan Exchange, was seriously injured in a taxi accident while on his first business trip to London. He remained in a coma until the following January, and has still to make a full recovery.

By then the overall corporate story had moved forward. Only a couple of months after joining up with Rowe & Pitman, Akroyd & Smithers had revealed the result of its own efforts to find an outside partner. In its case, Mercury Securities, the Warburg parent company, emerged as a 29.9 per cent stakeholder. These two firms already owned a business in New York to develop their trading of international fixed-interest securities, particularly in the Eurobond market.

Into the Nineties

Now that Rowe & Pitman was coming in with Akroyd, a three-way link was made, combining the Rowe & Pitman/Akroyd and Warburg/Akroyd joint ventures in New York under the revised acronym RoWaK (with a large 'W' to emphasize the Warburg link). This all made the question of Rowe & Pitman's future rather clearer. Given Wilmot-Sitwell's close relationship with David Scholey, Chairman of Warburg, no one was too surprised when, in August 1984, the three firms – Warburg, Rowe & Pitman and Akroyd & Smithers – opted for a full merger, bringing in also a fourth firm, Mullens and Company, the government broker, which the Bank of England was determined should share in the general bonanza. (In encouraging this four-way link, the Bank happily made its own facilities available for secret meetings.) According to Scholey, Rowe & Pitman's attraction to Warburg was that 'it was predominantly a corporate broker, with good international interests, and with a perceived compatibility of style, personalities and people'.

Thrashing out a deal, scheduled to be implemented in April 1986, a few months prior to Big Bang, was not always easy. Tempers became frayed as the four firms fought over their respective valuations in 'Newco', the original codename for what was officially known as the Mercury International Group (MIG). Rowe & Pitman (and its sizeable goodwill) was eventually valued at £60.4 million, or 14 per cent of the enlarged group. This was realizable in a cocktail of ordinary shares and highly geared warrants. The thirty-six partners could take £17.9 million out of the firm before the merger was finalized, but, as a form of 'golden handcuffs', conversion of deferred shares was not allowed before April 1989.

As for Charter Consolidated, it subscribed to bring its share in the overall group to 4.92 per cent, or 8.82 per cent after conversion. Initially it had wanted a much larger stake – as much as 30 per cent. But David Scholey, Warburg's Chairman, would not countenance that. He feared it would tar the new company with a South African image, which would not be popular in the United States. This attitude so annoyed Jocelyn Hambro, the Charter Chairman, that he threatened to unravel the whole deal.

Only some accomplished sweet-talking by Wilmot-Sitwell and Baring kept the deal on course.

One of Wilmot-Sitwell's specific concerns was ensuring that Rowe & Pitman's fund management business, Rowan Investment Management Services, also stayed on board. In the early 1980s, after James D'Albiac had exchanged his eyrie on the sixteenth floor of the Stock Exchange for an office at City Gate House, Rowan became a much more focused outfit, albeit one that often operated slightly at a tangent to the rest of Rowe & Pitman. D'Albiac's administration of local-authority pension funds was boosted when Cyril Jasper, formerly Treasurer of Hertfordshire County Council, was hired as a consultant in 1982. This paid dividends that same year when Rowan won control of the £30 million Northamptonshire pension fund. Meanwhile, at City Gate House, the hiring of David Boyle, a traditional fund manager, from Morgan Grenfell in October 1982, gave Rowan the know-how to operate similar-sized funds on behalf of Portals and Sainsbury.

If never a dizzily high performer, Rowan established a niche as a good and trustworthy fund manager. As a result total assets under its management grew from £17 million in 1976 to £287 million in 1982, when Ogilvy, as his contribution to the capital expansion exercise, started examining the possibility of selling part, if not all, of Rowan's equity. At one stage Dunbar, a private bank run by David Backhouse, looked set to take a 49 per cent stake in Rowan. This never happened, but the new Warburg link was perceived to pose new threats to Rowan's well-being. In particular, fearful that his side of the business would be swallowed up by Warburg's much larger Mercury Asset Management, Ogilvy made another bid for a Unilateral Declaration of Independence. However Wilmot-Sitwell was adamant that Rowan was not for sale, certainly not before Big Bang. During a golf match at Swinley Forest, he told D'Albiac bluntly, 'The merger has not been arranged solely for the benefit of Rowan executives.'

In the new environment of Chinese Walls, Wilmot-Sitwell and Scholey agreed that their own former companies' contributions to the investment management and corporate finance sides of the enlarged Warburg group should be run separately. (The new financial conglomerate soon reverted to its established Warburg name rather than the more prosaic MIG.) The Rowan identity continued within Warburg for a while in Mercury Rowan Mullens, which catered for private clients, charities and the old Rowan pension funds. In the event, this composite business did not last long when pitted against Mercury Asset Management. However, as a corporate broker, Rowe & Pitman more than held its own, the old name still attracting business from its traditional merchant-banking relationships.

Even before linking up with Warburg, Rowe & Pitman had decided to move yet again – this time, round the corner to the top two (sixth and seventh) floors of 1 Finsbury Avenue, the first building in the now well-known Broadgate Development. No longer was the firm content to carry on its operations from two separate premises. A futuristic, black glass-fronted building with large open areas around a central atrium, 1 Finsbury Avenue had been the brainchild of two Rowe & Pitman clients, Rosehaugh, headed by the Woolworth/Kingfisher entrepreneur Godfrey Bradman, and Greycoat. Under the auspices of Peter Hardy, Rowe & Pitman had arranged the finance for its development, bringing in the resources of British Land, Electra and Robert Fleming. Now, through his contacts, Hardy obtained an option on part of the building.

The new offices had to be fitted out with the latest information technology and dealing desks. However, despite their futuristic character – 'reminiscent of being on board an ocean liner' recalls one partner – traditions were maintained in a suite of three dining rooms, designed by Nina Campbell, for entertaining clients. In the main dining room Peter Wilmot-Sitwell insisted on the inclusion of a proper marbled fireplace.

However, shortly after moving in, Rowe & Pitman was exposed to an alarming bomb threat. John Littlewood, the former head of research, had been appointed Administration Partner when Alan Davenport retired in 1982. This was a job not normally relished by other colleagues but, after some twenty years of number-crunching in Research, Littlewood volunteered to take on the new challenge of responsibility for personnel, information technology, settlement, premises and administration. He was supported by a strong team of managers that included: Gordon English, the RHB stalwart who was Settlement Manager and Financial Controller of the new firm; Richard Steggle, who had joined from W.H. Smith to take control of systems development and operations; Alan Walsh, an expert in telecommunications, an increasingly important skill as the firm was expanded overseas; and Peter Smith, the former Office Manager who now specialized in personnel.

Littlewood was away from his office one afternoon in November 1985, when someone telephoned to ask for 'John Littlejohn'. Told that Mr Littlewood was not available, the caller stated peremptorily, 'The tape will be delivered in 25 minutes; listen to it.' Two subsequent messages asked, 'Well, have you found the tape?' Asked what was meant, the mystery voice replied, 'The tape in the bag.' It transpired that a bag containing a tape had been left in reception. The bag was quickly identified and, this being at the height of an IRA bombing campaign, the tape was played through. This revealed that a bomb had been inserted in a wall during the fitting out of the new offices. It would only be deactivated if a representative of the firm delivered a bag containing £300,000 in used notes. Since the caller had shown a detailed knowledge of the firm and its personnel, he was taken seriously.

A policeman was deputed to undertake the task. In best thriller fashion, he was instructed to go to a specific telephone box outside St Bartholomew's Hospital and dial a number, which then informed him to proceed to a rendezvous in the Barbican. His progress was monitored all the way by colleagues in the City of London Police and the Anti-Terrorist Squad. However, when he reached his next destination, a man popped out suddenly from a British Telecom tent in the road, grabbed the bag, and managed to evade all pursuers as he raced through the City's subterranean tunnels. Luckily the bag contained only a token amount of real money.

Following the 1985 merger, S.G. Warburg showed its commitment to Rowe & Pitman and the new venture by renting two additional floors in the same Finsbury Avenue block. Taking their lead from the two principals, David Scholey and Peter Wilmot-Sitwell, the two firms, with their seemingly disparate mixture of brokers, jobbers and merchant bankers, worked well together. They created a conspicuously happy environment – by far the most successful of the various City tie-ups which happened around Big Bang.

Only occasionally did the usual problems of large, diversified businesses intrude – as in September 1988, when Minorco, another financial holding company in the vast Anglo American group, mounted an audacious bid to wrest complete control of Consgold. When Minorco wanted Warburg's (essentially Rowe & Pitman's) broking team to work on its behalf, this created a potential conflict of interests, since the firm's corporate finance division had been asked to act for Consgold. To avoid any problems, Scholey insisted that Warburg should remove itself from the contest, and not act in any capacity for either Minorco or Consgold. Anglo American (and those close to it among the old Rowe & Pitman partners) were most put out. In the event, Minorco's bid for Consgold fell foul of US anti-trust law and, after a flirtation with James Capel, Minorco returned to the Warburg broking fold in 1996.

Unfortunately, even a company with Warburg's human and financial resources was not a big enough player to operate as a truly international investment bank in the 1990s. By 1995 the Swiss, Americans and Japanese carried all before them, and Warburg was floundering. The merged company looked to Morgan Stanley, an old Rowe & Pitman friend in the United States, to come to their rescue. In the event, assistance was closer to hand in the shape of an £860 million takeover bid from the Swiss Bank Corporation (SBC).

Active in the City of London with a traditional branch since 1898, SBC had stepped up its presence in 1979 when it also established a British-based investment bank, Swiss Bank Corporation International (SBCI), which dealt largely in international securities underwriting and the Euromarkets. Under Johannes de Gier, who was later to head the merged SBC Warburg bank in London, SBCI worked productively with Rowe & Pitman's Corporate Finance Department in capital market activities.

In the run-up to Big Bang in 1986, SBC, in common with its competitors, sought to rationalize its services while at the same time taking advantage of the new opportunities to supply an integrated range of financial services. In this spirit, SBC acquired a local stockbroker, Savory Milln, and brought together its various London operations in Swiss Bank House overlooking the River Thames.

Warburg at the same time was going through the same process. Without having quite SBC's global spread or capital resources, Warburg proved vulnerable to the pressures of the world-wide rise in interest rates in 1994, which caused a drastic cutback to its earnings from securities trading, without providing compensatory revenue from new growth areas like derivatives. However, if there was one field in which Warburg continued to excel, it was international investment banking. Its great strengths, such as its pole position in Germany's difficult Mergers and Acquisitions market, not only made it an attractive acquisition for SBC, but also ensured that it fitted well with the Swiss giant's broader-based business.

In the process, as S.G. Warburg was subsumed into the newly named SBC Warburg in May 1995, further traces of the old Rowe & Pitman inevitably disappeared. In 1996, the last trading company including the name Rowe & Pitman was closed down. Even then, the firm's reputation lived on. Its new owners were somewhat surprised to find that their most valuable acquisition was not, as they had been led to believe, Rowe & Pitman's corporate broking relationships, but an unparalleled distribution system, which had been tried, tested and perfected in the old Rowe & Pitman Operations Room. They also discovered the firm's spirit of friendly competitiveness: at the Rowe & Pitman pensioners' lunch in Finsbury Avenue in May 1996, Oliver Baring drew loud cheers when he announced that a large percentage of the new group's business had been won through old Rowe & Pitman contacts.

Into the Nineties

As Rowe & Pitman became a fond historical memory, questions were inevitably raised as to whether it needed to go this way. Might the firm have survived if it had acted more traditionally and avoided the markets' mad rush towards globalization? Its old rival, Cazenove, stood aloof from Big Bang, it was argued, and suffered little. The debate will continue, but it is hypothetical. For the London market was only ever likely to be able to support one large successful independent stockbroker after Big Bang.

By the 1980s Rowe & Pitman was not the firm to fulfil that role. But at the same time it was no longer the close-knit family club that had underwritten the lifestyle of Lancy Hugh Smith half a century earlier. Like the daily rounds of the merchant banks that brokers once made, an era had passed. Rowe & Pitman had developed into a solid professional financial organization – one that could operate equally well in the City of London or abroad, and one whose skills and contacts commanded an extraordinarily high premium in the new world of the 'all-singing all-dancing' investment bank.

Appendix I Partnership details 1894–1984

Born	Partner	Date of Entering Partnership	Date of Death or Retirement
1851	G.D. Rowe	December 1894	R 25.3.22
1863	F.I. Pitman	December 1894	R 28.3.40
1870	L. Hugh Smith	31.3.1898	D 23.3.41
1873	M.C. Pilkington	30.6.1899	D 26.6.26
1867	G.F. Watson	31.12.1902	R 25.3.22
1877	R.W. Cooper	30.6.1906	R 22.3.28
	J. Martin Smith	31.12.1913	D September 1914
	W.G. White	30.3.1917	R 22.3.28
1886	Hon. J.B. Lyon	30.6.1919 (sharing from 25.3.22)	D 7.2.30
1892	F.A.H. Pitman	25.3.1922	D 25.7.63
1892	A.F. Graham Watson	1924 (sharing from 2.4.25)	R 5.3.57
1892	S.R. Cooke	22.10.1925	D 3.7.30
1890	The Hon. A.A. Vanneck	31.12.1926	R 26.9.50
1898	F.J.P. Chitty	1928 (sharing from 22.3.28)	R 22.3.49
1895	The Hon S. Rodney	6.11.1930 (sharing from 23.1.31)	R 5.3.57
1886	A.E.D. Anderson	1.1.1931	R 5.4.66
1910	Hon H.V. Smith	12.4.1935	R 5.1.46
1908	I.L. Fleming	18.6.1935 (sharing from 1.6.35)	R 5.11.45
1914	E.C. Baring	12.11.1937 (sharing from 1.11.37)	R 25.9.51
1908	H.M. Bray	6.11.1945	R 5.4.61
1908	A.E. Leveson	6.4.1946	R 5.4.74
1902	W.J. de Knoop	6.4.1947	R 5.4.67
1923	J. Graham Watson	13.6.1949	R 5.4.72

Appendix I

7.6.16	J. Martin Smith	28.9.1949	R 10.4.79
1925	W.T. Henderson	27.9.1950	R 5.4.68
1903	T.C.G. Leveson Gower	26.9.1951	R 5.4.68
1926	G.W. Mackworth-Young	22.10.1953	R 27.12.73
4.12.23	R.N. Wadham	29.10.1954 (sharing from 23.3.55)	R 10.4.77
1.5.31	D.A. Innes	6.4.1958	R 6.4.84
1926	M.C. Bonsor	6.4.1958	R 30.6.71
5.3.27	W.R.D. Robson	6.4.1959	
28.3.35	P.S. Wilmot-Sitwell	6.4.1960	
7.1.22	The Hon. P. Vanneck	6.4.1961	R 10.4.79
31.8.30	D.S. Milne	6.4.1961	
26.1.27	R.T. Gibbs	6.4.1963	R 10.4.75
28.6.34	The Hon. James Ogilvy	6.4.1964	
25.8.14	W.J. Corney	6.4.1965	R 10.4.77
24.2.22	A.D. Davenport	6.4.1968	R 16.4.82
23.10.38	R.D.C. Brooke	6.4.1968	
14.10.35	J.C.R. D'Albiac	6.4.1968	
18.5.10	A.G. Little	6.4.1969	R 10.4.76
23.8.30	G.S. Finn	6.4.1969	
2.1.34	C.D.T. Fitch	14.4.1970	R 10.4.75
28.2.43	H.N. Verey	14.4.1970	
8.8.41	N.R. Elwes	5.4.1971	
15.8.30	D.I. Harding	5.4.1971	
1.4.43	D.I. Russell	13.4.1971	
9.12.35	M.F.M.O. Jodrell	5.4.1971	
17.11.30	R.W.D. McKelvie	5.4.1971	R 10.4.75
4.8.41	R.H.A. Southby	5.4.1972	
17.1.42	A.J. Radcliffe	5.4.1973	
8.9.44	O.A.G. Baring	10.4.1974	
21.12.31	P.E. Morley	10.4.1974	
27.12.20	A.D. Hurst-Brown	26.4.1975	R 16.4.82
11.3.27	J.A. Fergusson	26.4.1975	R 10.4.76
18.4.35	J.N. Littlewood	26.4.1975	
28.12.28	P.B. Hardy	26.4.1975	
4.7.20	J.D.W. Stobart	26.4.1975	R 11.4.80
2.11.33	D.A. Childs	26.4.1975	
26.7.36	A.O. Taylor	26.4.1975	
2.9.35	C.C. Surtees	26.4.1975	
13.5.09	G.A. Loveday	26.4.1975	R 25.7.75
9.8.44	S.R. Stradling	10.4.1976	
1.5.40	J.D.A. Wallinger	31.10.1976	
15.7.36	R.G. Newman	10.12.1976	

12.2.46	R.J. Rhodes	10.4.1977
3.2.47	A.R. Bonsor	10.4.1978
14.9.35	M.J. Franzman	10.4.1978
2.4.38	P. Heming-Johnson	10.4.1978
5.5.39	D.H. Back	10.4.1979
11.5.47	G.W. Pilkington	10.4.1979
26.5.36	P. Thompson	12.4.1980
10.6.43	H.T. Pelham	17.4.1982
12.3.40	E.R. Carbutt	17.4.1982
29.5.44	J. Appleby	17.4.1982
22.9.48	D.K.L. Ruck Keene	17.4.1982
19.5.49	M.J. Hesketh	9.4.1983

Appendix II Major Equity Issues, Vendor Placings and Sterling Bond Issues 1972–82

MAJOR EQUITY ISSUES

Date	Company	Issue	Sum Raised (£m)
2.2.72	BLMC	Rights Issue	51.5
15.6.72	Scottish & Continental Investment Trust	Offer for Sale	14.3
3.7.73	J Sainsbury	Offer for Sale	14.5
5.11.73	Christies International	Offer for Sale	5.3
6.5.75	Prudential Assurance	Rights Issue	47.7
12.5.75	United Biscuits	Rights Issue	14.5
20.5.75	Siebens Oil and Gas (UK)	Rights Issue	9.0
20.6.75	Legal and General Assurance	Rights Issue	24.7
24.7.75	Land Securities Investment Trust	Rights Issue	21.1
5.12.75	Plessey	Rights Issue	25.2
12.5.76	ICI	Rights Issue	203.1
13.7.76	Hambro Life Assurance	Offer for Sale	10.0
24.3.77	Prudential Assurance/Standard Trust	Cash Alternative	30.8
6.4.77	GKN	Rights Issue	66.8
20.6.77	BP	Offer for Sale	564.8
20.7.77	British Sugar Corporation	Rights Issue	18.8
10.10.77	United Biscuits	Rights Issue	30.7
19.10.77	IMI	Offer for Sale	68.0
8.3.79	Cement Roadstone Holdings	Rights Issue	30.2
18.4.79	Slough Estates	Rights Issue	24.8
22.5.79	Thomas Tilling	Rights Issue	59.3

From Diamond Sculls to Golden Handcuffs

31.10.79	BP	Offer for Sale	290.4
6.11.79	Thorn Electrical/EMI	Cash Alternative	102.7
5.12.79	Pilkington Brothers	Rights Issue	62.3
12.3.80	United Biscuits	Rights Issue	34.9
5.6.80	Land Securities Investment Trust	Rights Issue	108.3
21.5.81	Guardian Royal Exchange Assurance	Rights Issue	78.7
18.6.81	BP	Rights Issue	623.8
4.9.81	John Brown	Rights Issue	24.9
23.10.81	Cable and Wireless	Offer for Sale	223.9
15.12.81	ICL	Rights Issue	33.4
14.11.81	Habitat/Mothercare	Cash Alternative	40.3
19.1.82	MEPC	Rights Issue	64.4
29.5.82	Associated Heat Services	Offer for Sale	7.4
29.9.82	Paternoster Stores/F.W. Woolworth	Cash alternative	165.0

VENDOR PLACINGS

Date	Company	Sum Raised (£m)
31.12.75	Pilkington Brothers	2.2
18.12.76	United Biscuits	7.1
30.6.77	EMI	6.4
24.7.80	Greycoat Estates	1.2
6.11.80	Simon Engineering	2.1
7.11.80	Pritchard Services	2.3
5.1.81	Dalgety	9.9
19.3.81	Cement-Roadstone	5.6
5.6.81	Simong Engineering	1.5
7.5.81	Rosehaugh	1.4
17.8.81	Thomas Tilling	11.4
13.10.81	Tarmac	21.0
17.10.81	Pritchard Services	14.1
27.11.81	Dalgety	10.3
25.3.82	Thomas Tilling	26.2
21.5.82	Wolseley-Hughes	10.1
21.5.82	Mills & Allen	7.5

Appendix II

STERLING BOND ISSUES

Date		Borrower	Sum Raised (£m)
1981	January	Republic of Ireland	15
	March	Kingdom of Sweden	50
	April	World Bank	100
	April	Petroleos Mexicanos	50
	May	Hydro-Quebec	40
	September	United Mexican States	50
	October	Province of Nova Scotia	30
1982	February	Trans Canada Pipelines	25
	March	World Bank	100
	June	New Zealand	100
	July	Australia	100
	September	Hydro-Quebec II	50
	September	MEPC	30

Appendix III

IF by Bill Mackworth-Young

If you can keep your Shell when all about you
  Are cutting theirs and blaming it on you;
If you can trust B.P. when Arabs flout you,
  But make allowance for their flouting too;
If you are calm while all the City fusses
  And, in the fleeing crowd, don't take to flight;
Or, though disgusted, don't give up your Gussies,
  And yet don't feel too sure that W-lfs-n's right...

If you can live, and live without commissions,
  If you can smile, and not make smiling smug;
If you can look at charts and statisticians
  And spurn these two deceivers with a shrug;
If you can bear to hear your grounds for buying
  Twisted by bears to damn and disconcert,
Or watch the shares you've put your shirt on dying,
  And go and get yourself another shirt...

If you can heap your scant remuneration
  And risk it all on one despairing stag
And lose, and utter no recrimination
  To M-rg-n, or to L-z-rd, or to W-gg;
If you can force yourself to be a hero
  And grasp NChanga through the dancing years,
And so hold on when copper's down to zero
  And synthesis is harassing De Beers...

Appendix III

If you can talk with Saints, and keep your Burmah,
    Or walk with Tramps, nor lose your Royal Dutch;
If, while the market sags, your friends grow firmer;
    If jobbers count with you (but not too much);
If you can fill each agonizing minute
    With sixty seconds' worth of business done –
Yours is the Daily List, and all that's in it,
    And, which is more, you could be right, my son.

(With apologies to Rudyard Kipling)

Index

Abel Smith, Alex, 72
Akroyd & Smithers, 129, 137, 138–9
Aitcheson, Topeka & Santa Fe Railway, 33
Alliance Capital, 120
'aluminium wars', 73–4
Anderson, Arthur, 57–8, 60–1, 62, 68, 70, 73, 76, 92, 111
Anderson, John, 12
Anderson Strathclyde, 131
Andrews, Chris, 100
Andrews, Norman, 117
Anglo American Corporation, 64–5, 79, 87, 126, 128–9, 131, 137, 143
Argyll, 135
Ark Royal, HMS, 62
Ashman (senior boy), 29
Asquith, Margot, 37–8
Astaire, Adele, 72
Austin Friars premises, 22, 28–30
Australian United Corporation, 84

Balfour, Frederick, 23, 28, 30–1
Balfour Williamson, 23–4
Banister, Nick 138
Baraghanath, Laurie, 133
Baring, 11, 15, 18, 49, 103
Baring, Esmond, 58, 61–71*pas*, 78, 79, 80, 137
Baring, Guy, 58
Baring, Oliver, 87, 128, 131, 140, 144
Barnato, Barney, 11
Barnett, W.H.L. & Co., 12
Bates, Miss (telephonist), 100
Bearstead, Walter, 41
Beaverbrook, Lord (Max Aitken), 43, 48–52, 69–70, 94

Beckett, John, 123, 132
Begg, Gordon, 138
Beit, Alfred, 137
Benka, Herbert, 104
Bicester, Lord, 79, 99
'Big Bang' 1986, 134*ff*
Bishopsgate, 43, premises, 39, 62–3
Bishopsgate Within, premises, 22
Blitz, 62–3
Blue Circle Group, 25
Board of Management, 1974, 110
bomb threat, 1985, 142
Bonar Law, Andrew, 48
Bonsor, Michael, 71, 83, 89, 91
Bonsor, Richard, 86, 106
Bonsor, Susie, 86
Boothby, Charlotte, 22
Boothby, Robert, 22
Bowes-Lyon, Jock, 41–2, 57, 103
Boyle, David, 140
Bradman, Godfrey, 131–2, 141
Bray, Hilary, 59, 63, 64, 66, 70, 73, 75–6, 106, 111
British Aerospace, 134–5
British Aluminium, 73–4
British Bank of Northern Commerce, 39
British Metal Corporation, 15
British Petroleum, 123
British Sugar Corporation, 123
Britoil privatization, 134
Britton, Tommy, 27–8, 30, 55
Broadgate Development premises, 141
Bromley-Davenport, Edward, 112
Brooke, David, 82, 83–4, 87, 88, 89
Bucklersbury House, 75
Buist, Bob, 120, 121

Burmah Oil, 122
Burns, Walter, 16, 18, 33
Buxton, Sydney, 15

Camp Bird shares, 13, 19, 54
Campbell, Nina, 141
Canadian Agency, 34
Capel-Cure & Terry, 44
Carr, W.I., 86
Carson, Douglas, 95
Castlerosse, Viscount, 49
Cavendish, Lord Charles, 72
Cazenove, 22, 24, 57, 73, 83, 96, 145
Channon, Paul, 135
Chaplin, Milne & Grenfell, 33
Charles Barker, 110
Charter Consolidated, 131, 137, 139
Charterhouse Group, 79
Chase Manhattan, 101–2
Cherry-Garrard, Apsley, 43
Chiang kai-shek, 63
Chitty, Fred, 47–8, 66
Christie, Agatha, 43
Christison, McCulloch, 31
Churchill, Winston, 37
City Athenaeum, 11
City Gate House premises, 102
Clarke, Neil, 130, 137
Cleminson, Hugh, 36
Coates, William F., 100
Collier, Edward, 105
Consolidated Goldfields, 126, 128–30, 143
Continental Corporation, 127
Contraband Committee (Board of Trade), 37
Cook, Cyril, 100
Cooke, Sydney Russell, 44–7, 82
Cooper, Robert, 22, 25, 29, 36, 73
Corney, Bill, 60–1, 62–3, 71, 83, 95, 118
County Bank, 117
Coutts, 76
Craigie, Mrs, 107
Craven, W.T., 28
cricket, 103–4
cross-country running, 105
Cuckney, Sir John, 134
Cunliffe, Walter, 18, 24
Cunliffe Brothers, 23, 24, 73
Curacao, HMS, 62

D'Albiac, James, 78–9, 95, 96, 111, 121, 140
Daniell, Henry, 17, 35
darts, 105
Davenport, Alan, 95, 96, 97, 110, 111, 141
Davenport, Nicholas, 44–5, 46–7
Davis Borkum & Hare, 128
'dawn raids', 128–31
de Beers, 50, 64, 72, 87
de Gier, Johannes, 143
de Knoop, Wilfred, 66, 68, 79
Deterding, Sir Henri, 41, 47–8
Deutsche Bank, 88
di Giorgio, Ann, 83
Diamond Trading Co., 77
Distillers, 135
Donaldson Lufkin Jenrette, 120
Downer, Teddy, 100, 105
Dunbar, 140

Eddy, Prince, Duke of Connaught, 32
Egerton, Seymour, 76
Ellick, Phillip, 100
Ellison, Rev. John, 61
Elizabeth, H.M. Queen, the Queen Mother, 42, 76, 103, 107–8, 122
Eltis, Walter, 133
Elwes, Nigel, 86, 94, 110, 111, 114, 118, 123–4, 137
English, Gordon, 117, 142
Eton Manor Boys Club, 51
Eurobonds, 88–90
Evill, Annie, 107

Federal Supply & Cold Storage Co., 13
Ferguson, Tom, 97
Fergusson, Alastair, 112, 114
Fidelity Management Research, 84, 117
Finch, Jim, 100
Finn, Geoffrey, 97, 106
Fisher, W.D., 30–1
Fitzpatrick, Paddy, 133
Fleming, Ian, 58–60, 63, 66, 88, 106
football, 104–5
Forbes-Adam, General, 63
Ford Motors, 54–5, 77, 82
Franzman, Michael, 97
Fraser, Lionel, 74–5, 100

Index

Fruhling & Goschen, 17
Fry, Eric, 77

GEC, 127, 134
Garboldisham Old Hall, Norfolk, 57, 67, 103
Gaymer, Jack, 100
Gibbs, Anthony, 13, 19
Gibbs, Timmy, 99
Gilts department, 97–8
Gold Standard, return to, 1925, 40
golf, 106, 112
Gower, Lord Ronald, 31–2
Graham Watson, Fitz, 44, 61, 62, 66–71*pas*
Graham Watson, James, 22
Graham Watson, Jim, 66, 67, 68, 76
Grand Trunk Railway, 34–5
Grange Investment Trust, 40
Grant, Eddie, 72
Grenfell, Arthur, 33–5
Grenfell, Dick, 17
Grenfell, Teddy, 17, 33
Grenfell, Walter, 28
Grey, Lord, 33–4
Greycoat, 141
Guest, Keen & Nettlefold, 57
Guinness, 135
Gundy, Charlie, 72

Hall, Admiral Sir 'Blinker', 37
Hambro, Charles, 72
Hambro, Eric, 16, 36, 37
Hambro, Everard, 16, 39
Hambro, Jocelyn, 139
Hambro, Olaf, 16, 66
Hambro, Violet, 16, 20
Hambros Bank, 15–16, 18, 39–40, 66–7, 75, 79, 88, 117, 127
Harcourt, Lord, 79
Harding, Derek, 77
Hardy, Peter, 112, 122, 132, 141
Hargrave, Arthur, 62, 78
Harker, Arthur, 45
Harris Winthrop, 38
Harwood, Ian, 133
Hatry, Clarence, 56
Haynes, Clive, 97
Hays Wharf, 15, 27
Helbert Wagg, 50–1, 67, 74, 100, 112

Heming Johnson, Peter, 99–100, 106, 122
Henderson, W.T. (Peter), 70–1, 88, 119
Herbert, Lord, 72
Heriot, Walter, 17
Herrington, Kipper, 62
Ho, Douglas, 138
Hoare & Co., 114
Holmes, Errol, 72, 104
Hong Kong Land, 85
Hong Kong office, 86, 138
Hugh Smith, Arnold John, 72
Hugh Smith, Aubrey, 15, 37, 59
Hugh Smith, Humphrey, 15
Hugh Smith, John, 15, 21
Hugh Smith, Lancelot ('Lancy')
  early days, 14–26, 29
  character, 19–21, 57
  wartime activities, 36–41
  interwar years, 41–53, 103, 106
  death, 61
Hugh Smith, Mildred, 15
Hugh Smith, Olive, 15, 17, 58
Hugh Smith, Vivian, 15, 16, 34, 48, 58
Hurst-Brown, Alan, 113, 115, 127, 132
Hyam, M., Wholesale Clothing Co., 14

Imperial Tobacco, 73
Industrial & Commercial Finance Co., 67–8
Innes, David, 71–2, 97, 98, 99, 101, 110, 132, 136
International Investment Trust (IIT), 90
International Overseas Securities (IOS), 89–90
Iran, 87, 127
Iron & Steel Holding & Realisation Agency, 68–9
Irish Crown Jewels, theft of, 32

Jardine Matheson, 85
Jasper, Cyril, 140
Jay, Fred, 28, 100
John, Augustus, 44
Jones, Taffy, 62

'Kaffir' (South African) mining shares, 11, 100, 137
Kamenev, Leo, 45
Kern, Paul, 89

Keynes, J.M., 45
Kindersley, Hugh, 47
Kingsbury, Guy, 116
Kissel Kinnicutt, 31
Kinross, J.B., 68
Kitchin, George, 13–14
Kleinwort Benson, 118
Knight (messenger), 107
Kreuger, Ivar, 41
Kuwait Investment Office, 68, 72, 84, 113, 117–18, 132

Laing & Cruickshank, 114
Laurence Sons & Gardner, 57
Lazards, 47, 73, 79, 84
Leveson, Arthur, 64, 68, 78
Leveson Gower, Tom, 71, 76, 79, 80, 92, 104
Lewington, John, 77, 110
Linton Clarke, 31, 32
Little, Arthur, 60, 95, 101
Little, Harry, 27, 55, 60, 62, 65
Littlewood, John, 112, 113, 114, 141
Lobitos Oilfields, 24
Loder, Wilfrid, 12
London Australia Investment Co., 85
London Crematorium, 19
London Trust, 14
Longden, John, 105
Loveday, George, 112
Lovering, Miss (first female typist), 28
Lovesay, Joe, 27
Lucky Stores, 84

MI5, 45
McGeorge, Penny, 100
Mackworth-Young, Bill, 71, 76, 79, 81, 83, 85, 93, 96, 97, 106, 109–11, 126
Marks Bulteel, 13, 19, 34–5
Marlborough, Duke of, 42
Marnham & Co., 24
Martin, 'Ham', 112–13
Martin Smith, Audrey, 17
Martin Smith, Everard, 16, 19, 20
Martin Smith, Julian (i) 21, 25–6, 34, 36, 51, 103
Martin Smith, Julian (ii) 66–7, 78, 79, 83, 88–93*pas*, 102, 107, 110, 111, 114, 123, 125, 126, 130
Mason-Macfarlane, General, 63

Meaney, Sir Patrick, 133
Melse, Joe, 90
Mercury, Rowan Mullens, 141
Mercury International Group (MIG), 139
Mercury Securities, 135, 138
Merlin Fund, 113, 120
Merlin High Yield, 120
Merrill Lynch, 136
Messel, 114
Miller, 'Gertie', 55, 62
Milne, Denis, 89, 101–2, 106, 110
Minorco, 137, 143
Mok Ying Kie, 85
Monkhouse, Reginald, 83
Montevideo Improvements, 31–2
Moore-Brabazon, Derek, 112
Morgan, J. Pierpoint, 16, 18–19, 65
Morgan family, 16, 18, 33
Morgan Grenfell, 15, 16, 54, 65, 67, 71, 79, 80, 109, 111, 117, 126, 136
Morley, Peter, 99
Morrison, Charles, 25
Morton Rose, 33
Mullens, 40, 133, 139

Nathan & Rosselli, 71
National Westminster Bank, 12, 15, 39
Nationwide Building Society, 132
Nelke Phillips, 38
Newman, Robert, 17
Noble, Maria, 107
North Carolina, Bank of, 137
Norwegian Fish Committee, 37

OFS Goldfields, 65
office organization, early, 28–30
Ogilvie Thompson, Julian, 72, 79, 129
Ogilvy, James, 79, 80–1, 88–91, 102, 110, 114, 120–1, 140
Oil Committee (Admiralty), 37, 41
oil industry, 37, 41, 44, 47, 49–50, 68, 84, 111, 123, 134
Operations Room, 77–81, 95–7, 121
Oppenheimer, 68, 87, 137
Oppenheimer, Harry, 130
Owen, Bill, 62
overseas offices, opening, 81–8

Pacific Stock Exchange, 83

Index

Pahlavi Foundation, 87
Palmer, Bill, 55, 57, 60, 62, 69, 103, 107
Panmore Gordon, 12, 19, 89
Paternoster Stores (Kingfisher), 132
Phillips & Drew, 118
Pelham, Henry, 122
Piercy, Lord, 68
Pilkington, Alec, 124
Pilkington, Charlie, 14
Pilkington, George, 122, 124
Pilkington, Malcolm, 14, 22, 23, 25, 29, 38, 47, 123
Pilkington, Nigel, 138
Pilkingtons, 14, 23, 119
Pinner's Hall, premises, 22
Pitman, Frederick senior, 12
Pitman, Fred, 12, 22, 29, 31, 32, 38, 39, 47, 61, 106
Pitman, Helen, 12
Pitman, Hugo, 43–4, 46, 54, 59, 61, 62–3, 68, 76, 82
Plessey, 101
Ponsonby, Ashley, 113
Powell, Enoch, 107
Prescott, Cave, Buxton, Loder & Co., 12
Prudential, 123, 132, 134

Radcliffe, Tony, 97
Ramsay, John, 100
Rank Organisation, 134
Rankin, Lady Jean, 107–8
Rayment, Constant, 62, 78, 94, 95
Read Hurst-Brown, merger with, 112–117
Research Department, 76–7, 116, 121, 133
Revelstoke, Lord, 18, 49
Revertex, 131
Reynold's Metals, 73
Rhodes, Richard, 97
Rhys, Jean, 20–1
Ridley Smith family, 16
rifle-shooting, 105
River Plate & General Investment Trust, 14, 123
Robeco, 88
Robins, Will, 104
Robinson, J.B. 13
Robson, William, 71, 85, 86, 125

Rodney, Simon, 57, 69, 70, 84
Rogers, Reg, 62
Rosehaugh, 141
Rothes, Earl of, 85
Rothschild, 19, 118
ROWAK, 137–9
Rowan International Fund, 119
Rowan Investment Management Services, 121, 140
Rowan Securities Fund, 119
Rowe, Charles, 104
Rowe, George D., 12, 18, 22, 29, 32, 38, 39, 43, 44
Rowe & Pitman (Far East) Ltd, 86, 138
Rowe & Pitman Inc., 83–4, 138
Rowe & Pitman (South Africa) Pty, 87–8, 130
Royal Dutch Petroleum Co., 41
Royal Exchange Assurance Corporation, 48–9
royalty, dealings with, 42
Ruck-Keane, David, 138
Rushbrooke, William, 27
Russell, David, 84, 137, 138

Safeway Stores, 84
Sainsbury, 124, 140
St Olave's School, 27, 60
St Regis Paper Co., 125
Salomon Brothers, 137
San Francisco office, 83
Sargent, John Singer, 44
Saunders, Ernest, 135
Scholey, David, 124, 138, 140, 143
Schroders, 50–1, 80, 113
Scottish Provident Institution, 22, 23
Scrimgeours, 23
Sebag, Joseph, 97
Serocold, Claud, 24, 37, 73
Shackleton, Francis, 31–3
Shawcross, Lord, 130
Shawinigan Water & Power Co., 24
Shell, 41, 49–50, 73, 118, 123
Shephard, John, 133
Sheridan, Clare, 45–6
Shubrook, Ron, 62
Sikorsky, 134–5
skiing, 106
Smith, Constance, 17, 37, 39
Smith, Capt. E.J., 45

Smith, Hugh Colin, 15, 16, 18, 31
Smith, Hughie Vivian, 58, 65, 106
Smith, Peter, 95, 107, 142, see also Hugh Smith; Martin Smith; Ridley Smith
Smith St Aubyn, 19
Smith's Bank, 15, 39
South African office, 87-8, 130
Spencer, Earl, 72
sport, 103-6
staff bonus schemes, early, 28, 30
steel denationalization, 1953, 68-9
Steffenberg, Erik, 64
Steggle, Richard, 142
Stenhouse, 127-8
Stevens, John, 111
Stock Exchange Tower premises, 102
Stockdale, Sir Edmund, 112
Stradling, Stuart, 121
Stuart, Sir Campbell, 45
Stuart, Emily, 16
Stuart, Mary, 16
Suggia, Madame, 44
Sun Insurance Co., 23
Sweden, British Mission to, 1915, 36
Swedish Match Co., 41
Swiss Bank Corporation, 143-4

Taylor, Alan, 114
Thomas Tilling, 14, 68, 133
Thompson, Peter, 122
Thomson McLintock, 40, 77, 136
Threadneedle St premises, 22
Titanic, 45
Tobacco & Matches Control Board, 37, 41
Tods, Murray & Jamieson, 12-13
Tube Investments, 73

Union Bank of London, 39
United Asset Management, 84
University Boat Race, 12, 14, 29, 43, 48

Vanneck, Andrew, 47, 61, 62, 66, 118
Vanneck, Peter, 106, 118

Vansittart, Robert, 36
Verey, Nick, 111, 117, 122, 133
Vesco, Robert, 91
Vickers da Costa, 86

Wadham, Ro, 71, 79, 90, 110
Wagg, Alfred, 51
Wagg, Arthur, 19
Walker, Herbie, 82
Walker, Joe, 100
Wall Street Crash, 56
Walsh, Alan, 100, 142
Warburg, S.G., 74, 89, 124-5, 134, 135, 139, 141, 142-4
Warburg, Siegmund, 48
Watson, Guthrie, 22, 29, 36
Wedd Jefferson & Co., 14
Weinstock, Arnold, 127, 132
Weller, Nelson, 83
Weller, Norman, 138
Wernher, Julius, 137
Westland, 134-5
Westminster, Duke of, 42
Wethered, Roger, 72
Wharton, Edith, 21
Whitaker, Tommy, 112
White, Walter, 24-5, 34, 41, 45-6
White, Wilfred, 56
Wilkinson, Lawrence, 60
Williamson, Bert, 47
Willis & Faber, 116
Wilmot-Sitwell, Peter, 80-1, 96, 110, 121-41*pas*
Wilson, Comar, 65, 81
Wilson, Robin, 87, 88
Wimpress, Harold, 100
Wong, Pandora, 86
Wood Stuthers, 120
Woolf, Virginia, 45
Woolgate House, premises, 100-2
Woolworth, 131-2
World War I, 25-6, 36-8
World War II, 61-3

Yule, Sir David, 43